The Gardener's Garden

JERRY HARPUR · FOREWORD BY JOHN PIPER CH

DAVID R. GODINE·PUBLISHER·BOSTON

For Marjorie, Nick, Rob, Marcus and Daniel, with love

First U.S. edition published in 1985 by
David R. Godine, Publisher, Inc.
306 Dartmouth Street
Boston, Massachusetts 02116

First published in the U.K. by Penguin Books Ltd
Copyright © Jerald Harpur, 1985
Introduction © John Piper CH, 1985

LC 85-70144
ISBN 0-87923-580-2

First printing

Printed in the U.K.

Title spread: Tony Schilling's Henry Price Garden at Wakehurst Place.
Page 13: Christopher Grey-Wilson's garden at Hitcham.
Page 17: Ken Akers's garden at Great Saling.

Contents

THE Gardener's Garden

1 Ken Akers · Great Saling
2 Brian Arbon · Clare College
3 Peter Borlase · Lanhydrock
4 Tony Schilling · Wakehurst Place
5 Bill Hean · Threave
6 John Bond · Savill Garden
7 Eric Pymont · Gorsley
8 Dennis Smalley · Abbotswood
9 Archie Skinner · Sheffield Park
10 Alan Eason · Hadspen House
11 Marian Couchman · Westminster Abbey
12 Stephen Anderton · Great Comp
13 Clive Jones · Holme
14 Peter Macfadyen · Lanlivery
15 George Peeling · Peckover House
16 Martin Colledge · Logan Botanic Garden
17 Chris Grey-Wilson · Hitcham
18 Brian Hutchinson · Castle Howard
19 George Lovatt · Willoughbridge
20 Bob Barnes · Clapton Court
21 Martin Puddle · Bodnant
22 Ken Pearson · Cadogan Place
23 Peter Beagley · Hall Place
24 Fred Waite · Sandringham
25 Don Drake · Uxbridge
26 Stephen Beasley · Girton College
27 Robert Hall · Polesden Lacey
28 Ken Cotton · Pusey
29 Richard Staples · Heaselands
30 Ashley Stephenson · Hyde Park
31 Richard Ayres · Anglesey Abbey
32 Robert Mitchell · St Andrews Botanic Garden
33 Alan Mason · Harewood

Perth
Glasgow   Edinburgh
Carlisle
IRISH SEA
NORTH SEA
Liverpool
Manchester
Sheffield
Nottingham
Birmingham
Norwich
Cardiff
Bristol
Reading
LONDON
Exeter
Southampton

ENGLISH CHANNEL

Foreword

JOHN PIPER, CH

Anyone who has been to our garden at Fawley Bottom in the summer or autumn knows that we have won the battle against tidiness. When Jerry Harpur first came here, I quoted Jean Cocteau at him as he eyed the tumbling disarray – 'a little too much is just enough for me' – and he has never stopped quoting it back.

In any garden, manicuring is a dead loss; more often, excess means success and the understanding between the owner, who may or may not have his own flair and expertise, and his gardener, whether learned and full-time or a part-timer who mainly understands bedding plants and mowing machines, is crucial. At any rate, the Cocteau business, so he says, is one of the reasons why Jerry has given me the pleasure of writing a foreword to this book. It *is* a pleasure because, not only is he an old friend, but also a photographer I have long admired; and because he has an eye quite out of the ordinary for gardens and plants.

The notion of exploring gardeners' own gardens – what happens when there is no one else's will to satisfy or combat – is a brilliant one. Chefs, they say, like to eat both sparingly and plainly in private; not so gardeners. Some of them show an appetite in their own gardens as richly varied and ambitious on a small scale as they do in the splendid broader acres in their charge. But some have identified themselves so clearly with the gardens they are responsible for that they have made no separate personal garden to speak of and so, when the original plan of the book was modified to include both gardeners' own gardens *and* the gardens they look after, it seemed likely to make a much more representative whole. What the book does show is the extraordinary dedication that gardeners have, their love of plants and the skilful way in which they make the plants display their beauties and the beauty of stone and brick and the shape of the terrain.

It is significant that, when I asked about one or two gardens that I noticed had not been included, Jerry said, 'I didn't really find a gardener there who identified himself with the place,' and, of one garden, 'The gardener felt that he had not contributed enough creatively to justify his inclusion.'

Looking at these illustrations, one is aware of the Englishness of English gardens, of how they derive from all that has gone before, from Brown and Repton, who created a splendid and stately ambience for them, to Lutyens and Jekyll, who elevated the cottage garden to undreamed-of domestic grandeur and picturesqueness. Nor should we forget the lovers and breeders of plants and the ingenious designers of follies, bridges, boat-houses and canals, nor the architects of the houses themselves that shelter, or demand, or create an individual atmosphere for the gardeners to work in: the gardens of grey-walled medieval houses with arbour and dovecot, asking for topiary and views along main paths to distant long grass beyond the ha-ha; or the gardens of the sixteenth- or seventeenth-century brick houses with high walls or hedges, keeping the east wind from the roses and the lavender; or the gardens of great houses such as Vanbrugh's Castle Howard, or Clare College, Cambridge, with their great architectural settings. These for me are among the choicest Harpur pictures here.

Photographs of gardens do not always do justice either to the plants or to the plan, formal or wild or a mixture of the two. They are too often pictures of static objects, as if a garden were a tapestry or an outdoor room, furnished with trees and flowers, but not subject to changing light or mood or to the flattery of the perfect moment. Jerry Harpur has looked not once but many times at his subjects, and has used invention and imagination to discover the exact circumstances in which to take each photograph: at seven in the morning for the Westminster Abbey garden, when the early sun is streaming through the trees on to the dewy grass or, in Mr Pymont's garden near Ross-on-Wye, when the wind has turned a great flood of daffodil heads slightly away from the camera, so that the effect is of trembling life, or when cumulus clouds terminate a path that winds between two burgeoning beds, making drama instead of a garden cliché. When he takes a cottage garden, such as the freelance gardener's in the Lake District, one feels as if one is standing up to the eyes in the scented and varied mass, thanks to the cunning angle of the shot.

But with all this artifice in the use of the camera, he never allows one to forget the actual plants, which, because of the knowledge, love and patience of the gardeners, shine in the right place at the right time.

John Piper at Fawley Bottom.

Preface

It is said that the sense of smell is the most evocative of all and, certainly, it is the aromatic smell of boxwood which reminds me of the first garden and gardener I ever knew. Walter Fernall was gardener to my grandparents in the thirties at Burton Latimer, where the garden included four box-edged, yew-backed herbaceous borders. Watching him work there, black-waistcoated, with rolled-up, thin-striped shirtsleeves and a trilby hat, awakened my first interest in plants.

It is easy for me to go on thinking of professional gardeners as the employees of private houses. Fortunately there are still some, although there are fewer of them and they work with considerably reduced staffs. Such have been the effects of the social revolution and the greater interest in gardening that, not only does the freelance or jobbing gardener have more scope, but gardeners are increasingly employed by commercial firms, public bodies like parks departments, institutions like the botanic gardens or great organizations like the National Trust.

It so happens that the original inspiration for this book came from the garden of a country-house gardener's home in Essex. Driving back from photographing there one July morning, I had the idea of producing a book featuring gardeners' own gardens, called *The Professional Gardener's Garden*.

By the time I arrived home the title had become simpler and, with the interest of my publisher assured, I was at Castle Howard three days later discussing the idea with Brian Hutchinson, chairman and founder of the Professional Gardeners' Guild. While he offered as much help as possible, his first reaction was that not many gardeners had good gardens of their own!

After some research the reason became apparent: many put so much creative work into their employers' gardens that it is those which, in effect, become their own. More than one man uses his garden as his employer's plant nursery. Another, whose house is set in the corner of the big garden, is so devoted to it that he works from before seven until dusk most days of the year.

Nearly two hundred gardeners in England, Scotland and Wales were contacted for *The Gardener's Garden*, so it displays a cross-section of much that is good about the British professional's approach. The stories, told by gardeners from widely differing backgrounds, describe the development of gardens both private and public, belonging to cottages and great houses, and are more diverse than I had expected.

There is the army officer, for instance, who took early retirement to do a horticultural course before freelancing from his cottage on the edge of the Lake District. A charitable organization found a dedicated young horticultural graduate who has created their garden in Cornwall for the teaching and enjoyment of handicapped people. One successful head gardener began his career as a gold-leaf expert working on great London buildings.

However different from one another, all gardeners have one thing in common: they cannot help but become a part of the natural creative process, assisting nature

Early morning mist shrouds the unique specimen of *Magnolia* 'Albatross', raised by Peter Borlase at Lanhydrock.

with soil composition, cross-pollination, grafting, collecting, propagation, experimentation, conservation, plant association – and, more often than not, passing on their knowledge. In this way their own lives are enriched and the environment progressively improved.

The collectors (represented here by Grey-Wilson, Mitchell and Schilling) help to maintain the general excitement of gardening and are some of the most fully involved in the profession: newly found plants, brought back from remote locations, are propagated, sometimes in the botanic gardens, sometimes at home. To place the collectors' work in historical perspective, it was only about a hundred years ago that J. D. Hooker sent home the seeds of thirty species of rhododendron from a plant-hunting expedition in Sikkim. The genus was unknown to botany at that time, but so widely has it been cultivated and propagated that cultivars of it are seen to flourish in many of the gardens in this book.

As one head gardener remarked, 'Whatever the gardener's particular interest, there are few other professions in which career and hobby are so often combined.' It is entirely because of the interest and enthusiasm of the contributors and their families that it has been possible to produce *The Gardener's Garden*. Some of the most illuminating moments of the whole project have been at breakfast in the gardener's house following early-morning photography in the garden. At that time of the day, in that cleaner, softer light, before anyone else is about, it is possible to appreciate more fully what the gardener has achieved.

Some of the plants in our own garden are now happy reminders of the generosity of professional gardeners; most exchange plants between themselves but I am afraid that it has been a one-way traffic in my case – so far.

Most of the gardens may be visited, although not all; the dates and times of opening may be found in up-to-date lists such as the National Gardens Scheme's yellow book, the Gardener's Sunday organization's green book, and *Historic Houses, Castles and Gardens in Great Britain*.

It has taken just over two years to research, collate, photograph and edit *The Gardener's Garden*. I have thoroughly enjoyed it all and hope that you will just as much.

Jerry Harpur

Jerry Harpur
Chelmsford
February 1985

The Gardens

Saling Hall Lodge and Saling Hall, Great Saling, Essex

KEN AKERS

The creation of atmosphere is something I have cared about ever since I was a boy in East Ham, London, not just in gardening but in any of the small worlds that a boy builds around himself. Forty years on from 'Digging for Victory' with my wheelwright father, I have been involved for the last ten years with the completely differing atmospheres of two gardens in the north Essex countryside, one for my livelihood, the other for relaxation.

As Head Gardener to Hugh Johnson in the gardens of Saling Hall, my original interest in gardening has broadened, while my own garden has developed in a different style next door.

What would my father make of it? His hobbies included cabinet-making and water-colour painting but, sadly, he died when I was sixteen. Fortunately, his feeling for materials and his artistic sense were passed on to me and, on leaving school, I was apprenticed as a decorator and learned various techniques, including the use of gold leaf and sign-writing. This eventually led to work in distinguished buildings like the Houses of Parliament and royal residences and I discovered a great deal about architecture in general.

All of this, with my cycling trips into the country as a boy, was groundwork for my present job, which came about almost by accident. I became interested in alpine plants and rock gardening and then joined the Alpine Garden Society, visited the Cambridge Botanic Garden and read books by Alan and Adrian Bloom to find out how to use perennials and conifers in an interesting way. At about the same time, I started working for myself, building stone fireplaces in a

variety of situations, and this led to an interest in the use of stone in the garden.

Because we wanted a bigger garden, with room to develop our ideas, my wife Joan and I moved to Saling Hall Lodge, between Braintree and Dunmow; it is built in the Essex cottage style, with pargeted plaster walls. The house stands off-centre in its half-acre garden and is surrounded on three sides by the woodland of Saling Hall, with a minor road on the fourth.

The first nine months involved living with the site and evolving a garden design, and by autumn, we were ready for the first planting of the 'bones' of the garden. Leyland cypresses were planted along the hedge line to the north-east for shelter, and the south-east boundary was softened with silver birch, underplanted with a variety of shrubs. Conifers went in as individual specimens, for colour and form: *Juniperus* × *media* 'Pfitzeriana', with its low arching habit for ground cover; *Thuja occidentalis* 'Rheingold', nicely rounded, with gloriously bronzed winter foliage; *Chamaecyparis pisifera* 'Boulevard', one of the best blue, soft-foliage conifers, and *C. lawsoniana* 'Smithii', a pyramid-shaped Lawson.

The invitation from Hugh Johnson to take on his garden at Saling Hall came around this time. This also gave me the opportunity of becoming a member of the Professional Gardeners' Guild; the nearest I had been to working as a professional gardener so far had been some landscaping in various small gardens, but here I was offered a full-time job in a garden which is now well known to garden enthusiasts. Its

greatest charm is in the walled garden of long, brick-paved walks and beds of bright perennial colours: in two of these columns *Chamaecyparis lawsoniana* 'Pottenii' tower along the walls and gnarled apple trees, pruned to a mushroom shape, are set in the lawns. In the wider garden, where Mr Johnson had indulged his passion for all kinds of trees, we have also developed parts of it to include a rock cascade and a Japanese pool, and, more recently, replanted the water garden.

The water garden provided an ideal opportunity to put into practice much that I had learned from reading Gertrude Jekyll, more particularly her book *Wood and Garden*. In this romantic area, the brief was to replant for a tapestry of greens and colour, and I began by splitting up all the existing candelabra primulas (*P. bulleyana* and *P. florindae*) and sowed seeds of *P. sikkimensis*, which I raised in a damp bed at the Lodge. There are now also hostas, ligularias ('Desdemona', with red leaves

2. The water garden at Saling Hall.

and one called 'The Rocket', with tall yellow spikes), rheums and bergenias, all planted close together. I intend to use *Meconopsis betonicifolia* as soon as I can propagate them and another plant excellent in masses, the small, red-tipped, lilac-flowered spikes of *Primula vialii*.

Gertrude Jekyll pointed out that February is a good month to size up the garden, in a half light and the mist, to get the form. Certainly it is interesting at that time to look out from my sunroom, which overlooks the main plantings at the Lodge, and decide what should be added or deleted. The atmosphere of the garden is rarely better than in the early morning when there is unbroken hoar frost on the grass.

In my own garden, at the Lodge, I have created a natural, semi-woodland garden, the entrance to which is through a five-bar gate. To the left, and in the front of the house, is the oval

drive with a central lawn and here are two examples of plant association which I find particularly satisfying; *Clematis tangutica*, yellow, bell-flowered, scrambles over a greengage tree, and five silver birches are backed by the evergreen of a *Pinus sylvestris* to accentuate colour and form, small leaves against pine needles. Here also the rose 'Kiftsgate' climbs and hangs from the trees.

On the left of the house, between it and the road, bloom two mixed herbaceous borders and, on the right of it, there stretches a large expanse of lawn, which takes up two thirds of the garden. Here a sundial and a classical stone seat provide a touch of theatre; by the house is a terrace lined with fuchsias and geraniums in pots; stone sinks stand above a bed filled with alpines. Various climbers feature on the house walls – the combination of the rose 'New Dawn', pyracantha and the white *Clematis*

'Madame le Coultre' has been a particular success.

Beyond all this is the area where I have let my interest in plants take over, although in a disciplined way; the bog garden, the peat garden (set in a raised bed of peat blocks) and the rock garden run the width of the garden, one into the other, beyond a small lily pond, overlooked by a vast horse chestnut tree from next door.

A mass of smaller plants give colour from early spring to late summer beneath trees like the *Acer pseudo-platanus* 'Brilliantissimum' in the peat garden. This is a slow-growing, mop-headed maple whose leaves in spring are wonderful peach-pink. The peat garden is a good example of a small-scale area; five square yards contain peat-lovers like *Rhododendron impeditum* (with violet-like flowers), *R. yakushimanum* (pink in bud, opening to white) and *R. hanceanum* 'Nanum' (pale yellow

3.

blossoms). I am particularly fond of the small, yellow-flowered cultivars and of the trilliums (*T. grandiflorum*, white, and *T. sessile*, with marble foliage and mahogany flowers) and the low, white *Sanguinaria canadensis* 'Flore Pleno'.

The rock garden gives the impression of having always been there, an achievement in Essex. This began with a stroke of luck; a friend noticed that a Victorian house which was being demolished had a derelict rock garden with limestone pavement. We excavated eleven tons of first-class material, which was brought and carefully sited around the newly dug pond.

Ten years later, on either side of the path which runs through the rock garden, there flourish dwarf alliums, *Alchemilla alpina* (dwarf lady's mantle), *Viola labradorica* 'Purpurea', cyclamens, pinks, the mat-like *Gypsophila repens* and *Dryas octopetala* (a native of the European Alps) and the

unique blue of *Anemone blanda*, which spreads everywhere in March. These are complemented by the architectural forms of three small junipers, *Juniperus communis* 'Compressa', which are also suitable for troughs and sinks, and, over the path, the tall *Robinia pseudoacacia* 'Frisia' produces golden-yellow leaves in April.

The herbaceous beds are on two sides of the house and one screens the greenhouse. Saling Hall sparked off my interest in herbaceous plants; *Sedum spectabile*, herbaceous geraniums and a variety of hellebores are favourites, as well as plants like *Aster* × *frikartii* (at its best in the second year after splitting), and *Euphorbia polychroma*. Because I care about the conservation of native plants, leucojums, fritillaries and primroses grow by the hedge under the larches of the Hall.

Joan and I enjoy opening the garden to visitors and, when I am preparing a

new season of garden talks, going through the colour slides of the past year, it gives me a great kick to check the development of the garden; this helps to keep the planting composition right.

3. The May morning light picks out the colours of the dwarf rhododendrons in the peat garden at Saling Hall Lodge, including 'Princess Anne' (yellow) and 'Humming Bird' (red) and the azaleas 'Hinomayo' (pink) and 'Gaiety' (pale pink).   4. November sun highlights the effect of frost on *Sedum spectabile* 'Autumn Joy' and, in front of the yew hedge, the branches of *Magnolia stellata*.   5. Naturalized clumps of *Crocus tomasinianus* and various snowdrops abound throughout the garden.   6. *Fritillaria meleagris*, a native British plant, thrives best in damp soil.   7. Summer in the limestone rock garden shows off a successful association of shrubs and perennials including the yellow *Iris pseudacorus*, the low-growing pink *Saponaria ocymoides* and the white *Arenaria grandiflora*; farther back are *Acer japonicum* 'Aureum', *Iris sibirica* and the *Acer pseudoplatanus* 'Brilliantissimum'.

20

4.

5.

6.

7.

21

The Fellows' Garden, Clare College, Cambridge

BRIAN ARBON

I first came to work in Clare College gardens in August of 1951, having just left school and not really sure that gardening was what I wanted to do. The knowledge and influence of the then head gardener, Walter Barlow, was quickly to make me realize that I had, indeed, done the right thing and that Clare gardens in their wonderful setting on the banks of the river Cam were to become the love of my working life.

The present layout of the gardens dates from 1946, when a group of Fellows, headed by Dr E. N. Willmer, was given the job of replanning the gardens after the neglect suffered during the Second World War.

At the very start it was decided that we should only grow plants that were suitable to our soil and growing conditions. The site was of just over two acres, and had consisted of an orchard

1. Brian Arbon in the garden by Clare Bridge.

and vegetable garden with a large herbaceous border running diagonally across the garden. The whole was fronted by a lawn which swept down to the river's edge. The Fellows' Enclosure ('Pond Garden') in the centre, enclosed by a tall clipped yew hedge whose dark leaves give such a wonderful background to brilliantly coloured flowers, is much sought after by drama societies, but the damage to the grass means that we have to turn down many of these requests.

As herbaceous borders take up such a large area of the garden, a great deal of time is spent over the whole year in their care, starting in December when the beds are all mulched in compost. This consists of our leaves, grass cuttings, and soft-stemmed plants which have been rotted over an eighteen-month period and when applied to the borders gives that rich black mulch look; it is very satisfying to know that you are putting back all your past rubbish into your own garden again.

The borders are all dug over to a good spade depth, and many plants are removed every year, so that they can be divided and controlled and replanted in groups of five or seven, the important thing here being that each plant has its own little area of garden to grow in. The hoeing which commences in early March makes it fairly easy to keep weeds under control. During the parts of the winter when, through heavy frost and snow, we are unable to work on the borders, attention switches to the removal of all the dead wood in the yew trees that surround the garden. These prunings are trimmed to make supports for other plants at the early stages of

their growth. Of course we use bamboo canes, too, but how much more pleasing to the eye are the yew trimmings.

Great care is taken in the blending of colours, and our biggest planting area consists of two wide borders with a centre walk where all plants are chosen to be yellow-to-gold and blue. Large groups of delphiniums sometimes 10–12ft high are flanked by verbascums, thalictrums (with wonderful grey foliage and lemon-yellow flowers), *Anchusa* 'Royal Blue' – what a true blue this is – heleniums, heliopsis, salvias and, coming on to the front, daffodils underplanted with violas in the spring, which are replaced when their foliage dies down in the early summer with *Tagetes* 'Lemon Gem', thus ensuring that at no time need there be any ugly gaps. Quite a large area on the front of the border is changed for spring and summer plants; last year we grew around 15,000 plants for bedding throughout the garden. The back of one side of the yellow–blue border has a high wall which supports ceanothus and roses. In the nearby corner, there is a large specimen of *Buddleia alternifolia* which dips its arching branches on to a large golden privet, giving a wonderful effect at flowering time.

Overlooking this part of the garden and surrounded by some large hazel trees is a *Metasequoia glyptostroboides* which was planted in the late 1940s, one of the first to be grown in this country. One of my earliest memories concerning this tree was pruning it when it was no higher than I was. Now it is over fifty feet high.

At the river end of the yellow–blue border stands a very good specimen of

Aesculus glabra, the Ohio buckeye, with its lemon-coloured flowers and its flame-red foliage in the autumn. At one time the area was being replanned, but the gardener who was told to clear this part of what was then a very overgrown garden felt that this tree was something special and spared it. We have much to thank him for.

At this part of the garden, we come to what must surely be everyone's idea of heaven on earth, for we have the river and, looking towards Clare Bridge with its near-Chinese serenity, a very large copper beech; peeping over the top are the magnificent towers of King's College Chapel. In the shadow of Clare Bridge is a *Cercis siliquastrum* (Judas tree), probably one of the oldest trees in the garden; over the years it has frequently been wired and propped to stop it committing suicide by dropping into the river. Its pea-like pink flowers in spring and, later, its red seed pods are a joy to behold.

The two large island beds which run by the river path are planted so as to give an increased sense of distance when viewed from Clare Bridge. This is done by blending the colours. We start at one end with pale orange flowering plants and then slowly deepen them with oranges and scarlets, finishing with crimson. In late summer and autumn, these two beds reach perfection, with dahlias dominating the centre, surrounded by groups of perennials and numerous clumps of red and orange annuals; towering over the whole garden river bed is a *Taxodium distichum* (swamp cypress).

The river, which is such an important part of the overall beauty of the gardens, can sometimes become our biggest cause for worry. Flooding is a constant threat, the last time being in May 1978 when the whole garden was under water and tulips were transformed into waterlilies overnight. This episode provided very good pictures for the army of photographers who descended on the garden, but was sheer heartbreak for a gardener. When I was called from home, the sight that greeted me was of a boat sailing down the main lawn, and I must admit to shedding a few tears.

The border that fronts the main lawn is planted with a mixture of colours backed by shrubs such as gold and silver privets, bamboos and hazels. Good effects can be achieved by the use of plants in front of the appropriate foliage. The lawn that runs the whole length of the garden has a slight change of level at about half way, and when viewed from the river end again gives the garden that longer-than-it-is look. During the summer, the thousands of overseas visitors are fascinated by the light and dark striping left by the cut of the mowers, almost as if it had been done with a paint brush.

At the far end of the lawn lies a small bed with a cupressus at the back. A few years ago during a storm it blew over and was only saved from going flat by leaning at a crazy angle on a neighbouring shrub, but with the help of a few willing pairs of hands it was pulled upright and held in position by props and wires; it now dominates a bed planted with lime-green nicotiania, *Cineraria maritima* and ageratum, and the combination of these plants gives an effect of true peacefulness.

Walking off the lawn and down a tunnelled walk of yews, we come to the Scented Garden where a great effort is made to ensure that perfume wafts over the rest of the garden for as much of the year as is possible, starting with two fine shrubs, *Chimonanthus praecox* and *Viburnum bodnantense*, which do much to brighten up the garden in the depths of winter. This is followed by a succession of shrubs, bulbs and plants, and three large beds in which annual stocks, heliotrope, verbena and dianthus are planted: in fact anything that gives even the slightest hint of perfume will find a place in this garden. Over the hedge there is my favourite tree of the whole garden, a *Tilia petiolaris* (weeping lime), with its silver leaves which rustle in the early summer wind, followed by its almost overpowering clover-scented flowers and, as if that is not enough, its wonderful golden leaves in the autumn. Every large garden should have one of these.

Just over the hedge from the Scented Garden is the nursery garden in which cut flowers for college functions are grown and plants raised for the main gardens. I have one big complaint here: IT ISN'T LARGE ENOUGH – so much so that whenever something dies, it's not uncommon for it to be pulled out in the morning and something else planted in its place by the evening.

2. The yew-enclosed Pond Garden becomes an open-air theatre in summer.

3. Daffodils and as yet unopened flowers of *Anemone blanda* soon after sunrise on either side of Clare Avenue.

5.

4.

Running the length of the garden on the opposite side from the avenue, under a row of very mature yews, is a border of shrubs and plants where everything is white. This is known as Telfer's Walk after an earlier Dean of the College, who would spend hours pacing up and down rehearsing his sermons. Where could be better on a summer's evening, with the coolness of the white flowers against the dark leaves of the yew, and in June the strange bracts of the ghost tree, *Davidia involucrata*?

6. The architectural shapes of King's College Chapel are repeated by the spires of *Verbascum* 'Gainsborough' in the yellow and blue border; here also are yellow *Thalictrum speciosissimum* and Pacific Hybrids of delphinium.

7.

8.

4. Dean Telfer's Walk is Clare's white garden; in June, white bearded irises, *Rubus* × *tridel* 'Benenden' and *Syringa* 'Madame Lemoine' catch the soft evening light.   5. In this part of the red border, *Nicotiana* 'Crimson Rock' grows in front of *Helenium* 'Moerheim Beauty' and *Nicotiana* 'Crimson Bedder'.

7. This specimen of *Cercis siliquastrum* (the Judas tree) is one of the oldest trees in the garden.   8. Clare College Garden flowerbeds are very large and varied in their planting. Marigold 'Seven Star', backed by *Penstemon* 'Bouquet' and *Dahlia* 'Bishop of Llandaff' are massed in the near bed, while *Salvia* 'Blaze of Fire' and *Rud-beckia* 'Marmalade' lead in to the main lawn.

25

1. The gatehouse in the formal garden as seen from the woodland garden.

Lanhydrock, Bodmin, Cornwall

PETER BORLASE

Gardening must have been in my blood. My grandfather was gardener on one of Cornwall's famous estates; my father was a carpenter, but also a beekeeper and very keen on his garden, and loved trying his hand at grafting – with a reasonable amount of success as I recall.

I am told I made my first attempt in horticulture at the early age of four. To my father's dismay, I removed all those beautiful shoots from his much treasured 'Sharpes Express'! Fortunately for me he was a very placid man. At the age of twelve, while at school, we were given a plot of land each and encouraged to 'dig for victory'. Perhaps most encouragement came from our schoolmaster, who was also a beekeeper–gardener and a friend of my father's, so I had to do my very best. I can remember carrying home a rake and hoe, the prize for one of the best plots. I think my mother then gave me a *New Gardening Encyclopaedia*. With all this backing, I started growing vegetables – flowers were for cissies.

2. Peter Borlase with *Magnolia × soulangeana*.

I started work in a garage to be a mechanic, and then I was called up for National Service. The latter was probably the best thing that could have happened, as on my return from my stint I was offered a job as gardener with the Copeland family at Trelissick, where I spent some twelve years.

I can well remember my interview with the head gardener, a Mr Julian, who took me through the glasshouse section and in the last house gave me a watering-can and said, 'Show me how you would water these plants.' Needless to say, these were all in clay pots, so I walked slowly along tapping each pot and watered only the pots giving a nice clear ring. 'That'll do, boy,' he said, and added, 'Do you shoot?' 'Yes, sir,' was my eager reply. So, as we left the walled garden for a tour of the gardens, he collected a single-barrelled shotgun from his office and handed it to me, with one cartridge, and muttered, 'We'll see how good you are.' As we walked along side by side a wood-pigeon flew out from some trees and away from us. 'Shoot it,' he yelled. Luckily for me I did, and without further ado I was taken before the 'old man', as they called the boss, and was asked to start the following Monday. Had I missed that shot I might never have had the job!

During the early years I attended evening classes to learn some of the basic principles of horticulture. Even now, with thirty years' experience behind me I can still feel like an apprentice at times when seeing a new plant; there are so many avenues to follow and we are all enthusiasts in different fields. Camellias have always been a great favourite of mine and this is reflected in the garden here at Lanhydrock. When I came here in 1966 there were some fifteen to twenty varieties, and now there are approximately 250 different cultivated varieties.

In the autumn of 1966 I was fortunate enough to take over Lanhydrock. Lord Clifden, who had given the property to The National Trust in 1954, had just died and his head gardener was ill, so it was then a beautiful but much overgrown garden. I was more than pleased to take up the challenge and fortunately the surviving sister, the Hon. Everilda Agar-Robartes, was most cooperative, and delighted to think the garden was to be taken in hand again. My predecessor's health improved sufficiently for him to help for a couple of half days a week, and, as he had been in the garden for some thirty-three years, I could have had no better help – for which I shall always be most grateful.

Magnolias are a main feature of the garden – there are large trees of *M. campbellii*, *M.c. mollicomata* and *M. veitchii*, which were planted by George Potter (the previous head gardener) in 1933 – his very first year at Lanhydrock. These trees are a magnificent spectacle each spring and I cannot imagine the garden without them. To ensure that they continue to be a feature here we have, over the past fifteen years, planted many more tree magnolias. These include the beautiful *M. mollicomata* 'Lanarth', *M.* 'Charles Raffill', *M. sprengeri* and *M. dawsoniana*.

3. Peter Borlase varies the summer bedding in the parterre garden each year. Surrounding the bronze urn are *Begonia semperflorens*, salvias, marigolds and antirrhinums.

4. Borlase's Stream, above which stands the thatched cottage, is abundantly planted with *Primula pulverulenta* and *P. japonica*; *Rhododendron cinnabarinum* 'Lady Chamberlain' stands to the left.

Storms can cause many a heartache, but sometimes when a large tree crashes down on to several precious plants, the gardener can seize the opportunity to plant other treasures. Borlase's Stream, with its primulas, astilbes and many other moisture-loving plants, might not have been created but for a monsoon a few years ago. A stone culvert that carried water from the well under the garden to the park was blocked, and to control the water I brought it to the surface with a few large stones, so that the water now flows over these. What better than the sight and sound of running water flowing below towering magnolias? Many a visitor stops in his track to take a second look.

A semicircular herbaceous garden with a tumbledown glasshouse and potting-shed to one side used to look quite a spectacle when the clematis and climbing roses were in flower, contrasting with the purple leaves of a vine which was draped over the unsightly brickwork. To re-move this group in order to make the garden a complete circle seemed a shame, but now, after ten years, the new yew hedge has grown to match that on the other side, and the plants within have matured to form nice groups and clumps; and many people return to see what they have missed on previous visits.

It has been said a garden should remain the same. I agree that the landscape should not be altered, but surely the face must change?

As mentioned, Lanhydrock's main features are the magnolias, and also the hardy hybrid rhododendrons, evergreen and deciduous azaleas, and camellias. The garden can be split into three main areas. By the house is the formal garden, the feature here being the Irish yews or *Taxus baccata* 'Fastigiata', which need clipping and tying at least once a year; I like to clip them in late July to August – late enough to clip the current year's growth, but early enough to allow any secondary growth

5. The circular herbaceous border, enlarged by Peter Borlase, flowers successively from June to October; here, in July, are *Acanthus spinosus*, several cultivars of hemerocallis, including 'Stafford' (bright red) and 'Flava' (yellow) with, in front of the wistaria-covered barn, the rose-pink *Anemone japonica*.

to harden before the onset of winter. A light dressing each spring helps make the right amount of growth and an occasional handful of medium or coarse bonemeal helps them keep healthy looking. These yews, planted around 1857, were a haven for jackdaws when I arrived, and were full of holes and nests. By filling in the holes with stiff wire netting and firing a cannon from time to time, we have persuaded the birds to take to the woods and avenue for their nesting places. Also within the formal area is the parterre, which has spring and summer bedding; the remainder of the beds are planted with roses, which give another marvellous splash of colour in midsummer.

The second area is the informal garden, with its magnolias and rhododendrons and many other shrubs.

The third area is the woodland, with its canopy mainly of English oaks, with rhododendrons and deciduous azaleas and a carpet of ferns throughout the

summer. I have added to this section quite a number of the large-leaf rhododendrons and *Magnolia* 'Charles Raffill', which seem to be doing very well in this situation.

The National Trust Gardens Adviser visits most properties at least once a year to discuss any problems, mainly those of a technical nature; the Trust's Regional Director is also present. Usually points of view are aired, discussed and agreed – although it is not always that simple, of course! Should any one of us feel very strongly on a particular point, there is usually a very good reason behind it and a gentlemanly agreement has to be reached.

Apart from gardening, I am interested in all things akin to the countryside. I raise game, which to me is much like growing chrysanthemums – a whole year's work but well worth while. I enjoy the shooting, but far more I like watching my pair of excited springer spaniel bitches with their noses

close to the ground and their tails wagging faster than any windscreen wiper when they flush their quarry. The feeling of fresh air and freedom when beating through the rough is total relaxation, although at the end of the day exhaustion would be nearer the truth. Just to walk through the woods and along the river bank taking in the beauty of the trees and the wild life – what more could a man ask for?

Unlike the Professional Gardeners' Guild, who meet at least once a year, the National Trust's Head Gardeners' Conference is held triennially. These meetings are basically educational, with lectures from the Gardens Adviser or a representative from a leading chemical firm, but consist mainly of good general discussion, where any grievance can be aired and, more important, there can be an exchange of views and knowledge. What a vast wealth of knowledge there must be at such a meeting of professional gardeners.

Royal Botanic Gardens, Kew (Wakehurst Place), Ardingly, Haywards Heath, West Sussex

TONY SCHILLING

Gardening at Wakehurst Place is a professional responsibility where most, if not all, of my duties fall under the cloak of management. I have nearly five hundred acres to cope with, for Wakehurst is a great undulating plot of plants. This ranges from exotic giant redwoods to the native prostrate wild thyme, from secluded walled gardens and spacious manicured lawns, through deeply wooded ravines to the open meadows, marshland and forest which collectively make up the Loder Valley Nature Reserve.

To make this great variety of vegetation manageable as the annexe garden of the Royal Botanic Gardens, Kew, I have a staff of thirty talented gardeners to back me up and to follow my pointed finger; a left-hand index finger which seems to spend much of its working life gesticulating in the direction of a necessary maintenance task or a new development project either of which may

be needed to improve this lovely garden in the High Weald of central Sussex.

When I go home to my flint-walled, hung-tiled nineteenth-century cottage which nestles close to the northern escarpment of the South Downs, I travel from a pH of 4.7 to one of 8.5, driving from a slow-draining silt-loam to a fast-draining alluvial outwash soil; I pass from vast acres to a percentage of just one, and leave behind a large staff of obliging colleagues to be met at home by a faithful dog plus a loving wife who gives me a quizzical look when I talk of the next gardening task. The contrast is amusing and one has to adopt a very different philosophy in order to assume the role of a domestic gardener with a staff of none. The 'manager's hat' is flung to the winds, off comes the jacket and tie and on go the old clothes; within minutes I've got soil behind my nails, including the one on my left-hand index finger.

As a teenager I struggled to achieve my initial horticultural aspirations on the heavy clay of surburban Middlesex. However, one of my earliest dreams was to live in the country in an attractive cottage, set on an easier soil with honeysuckle around the windows, rambling roses above the front porch and clematis over the woodshed. Happily I have been fortunate enough to realize that long-nursed desire.

The traditional English cottage garden, which appeals to so many, is without doubt one of the facets of horticulture I enjoy the most and by some fortunate twist of fate I can now indulge my romantic yen for this fascinating form of garden art both professionally and domestically.

At Wakehurst Place, we have during the last twenty years created and developed, amongst many other projects, the Henry Price Garden. It is a secluded garden with walls of mellow sandstone and Ashdown brick and is ornamented with wrought-iron archways, stone vases and a lead cistern. Since its conception, the Henry Price Garden has been given various flattering titles, such as 'a modern cottage garden' and 'an essay in colour'; both of these are apt, precise and descriptive. The effects throughout are soft and mellow as all hard colours of the spectrum have been excluded. In consequence nothing can jar on the eye, for all within these four walls flows and merges together in gentle harmony amidst a predominance of silver, grey and grey-green foliage. It is perhaps unique in content, including not only the traditional and well-loved plants of the English cottage garden such as sidalcea, dianthus, nigella,

1. Tony Schilling admiring the flower panicles of *Catalpa spinosa*.

Lavatera, delphinium and phlox, but also recently introduced exotic herbs and shrubs of botanical value such as *Salvia castanea*, *Daphne bholua* and *Ozothamnus hookeri*, and rare British native plants, including *Geranium sanguineum lancastrense* and *Althaea officinalis*. Although there is something of interest for every season it is designed as a summer garden and is at its best in August and September. Here, the art and science of gardening blend together to delight the senses and interest the inquisitive.

In the informal setting of the Himalayan Glade at Wakehurst we practise a very different gardening philosophy, namely that of representing an ecological association of plants native to the temperate and sub-alpine zones of the Himalayan mountains.

This dramatic feature is situated halfway down the deep ravine-like Westwood valley, an area with bold bluffs of Ardingly sandstone, steep slopes of opposing aspects and a deep stream bed. The glade has been planted with a mass of dwarf barberries including *Berberis wilsonae*, *B. angulosa* and *B. concinna*, and amongst this thorny sea of shrubs an occasional break of theme is created by isolated specimens of *Juniperus recurva*, *Cotoneaster microphyllus* and *Viburnum grandiflorum*, each offering a contrast in texture, habit and form. The slopes above and behind the glade are furnished with an informal mass of Himalayan trees and shrubs which add to the natural framework given by large rhododendrons lower down the slope, and over the rocks bold group plantings of different alpine bistorts have been made, including *Polygonum vacciniifolium* and *P. affine*.

In contrast to the many challenges that Wakehurst offers me, gardening at home is a relaxing activity, where I can escape from all management stresses and office commitments. At home I cultivate my garden for personal satisfaction and for therapeutic reasons, while at Wakehurst I manage the garden out of enjoyable but professional commitment.

2. Wakehurst Place mansion glimpsed through mature rhododendrons and American swamp cypress.

What I choose to grow in my private garden is decided by several factors. Firstly the light alkaline soil rules out all acid-demanding subjects, but this can be turned to advantage by growing plants such as dianthus, a genus which frequently sulks at Wakehurst. The same can be said of scabiosa, cistus, lavender and artemisia species. I've always believed one should find out what grows well on a given soil and then grow plenty of it. If it fits the cottage-garden theme then so much the better, for I enjoy above all else the constant search for a balanced picture composed of the innumerable forms, textures, habits and colours of plants. I also like to grow some of the species I have personally collected around the world during my many exploratory plant-hunting travels. Cistus and phlomis bring back memories of sunny days in the Mediterranean areas, *Eryngium planum* reminds me of happy times in the meadows of south-east Poland, and *Potentilla arbuscula* of demanding days on the lower slopes of Everest in the distant Himalayas. During one of my many Nepalese mountain treks a wag in our party suggested that having done the two-hundred-mile walk to Everest and back for four consecutive years I might consider myself to be in a rut. I remember pausing to reflect on this and, gazing at the overwhelming majesty of our surroundings, decided that if indeed I was in a rut it was certainly a most impressive one!

Like all true gardeners I'm always glad to accept plants from friends and neighbours and these when established become a sentimental link with the person who presented them to me. If I add the opinion and interests of others, namely my wife, to the reasons for domestic plant selection, then matters become still more involved. Annie is a botanical artist and has many an idea linked to a current or future artistic need. She has an incredibly keen eye and a sharp perception and what is ordinary to me is often wildly exciting to her. Possibly only she would be actually happier to sit down and draw a Savoy cabbage rather than stand up and cook it, and only she could persuade me to cultivate and nurture couch grass so that she can paint it for a field guide. Even our hybrid corgi, otherwise known as the 'bonsai Alsatian', has a direct influence on the garden's content. Having no really secure boundary fence we are obliged to tether him on lazy summer days to an *Escallonia* 'Apple Blossom' – yet another example of plant form and function!

Which of my gardens gives me most pleasure? This is a basically unanswerable question, for as long as one is involved in creating a living landscape and working with plants it matters little whether the acreage is great or small or the pH is high or low. On the one hand my cottage garden gives me great domestic satisfaction and the results are enjoyed by family, friends and neighbours, but by the same token Wakehurst gives me immense professional gratification and affords pleasure to a great many.

I realize that what others describe as my natural enthusiasm coupled to considerable impatience gives me a reputation for being a demanding task master, but in truth I am even harder on myself, believing that there is surely little merit in endeavour if it is not directly linked to a desire to seek high standards. Given the necessary resources, a good garden is not too difficult to create, but a really great garden demands a total commitment.

The end hopefully justifies the means and the rewards are many, not least of these being the enjoyment Wakehurst gives to the 125,000 or more visitors who pass through its gates annually. They come seeking many things including gardening inspiration, peace of mind and intellectual stimulation, but most of all I believe they come in quest of beauty.

3.

4.

3. In July Tony Schilling's Sussex cottage garden overflows with hemerocallis, delphiniums, phlomis, alstroemeria and anthemis.
4. Morning in the walled garden with the pink flowered *Ceanothus* 'Marie Simon' dominating the foreground.   5. Stone vases seem to float on the purple haze created by the sixty-metre long hedge of *Lavandula* 'Hidcote'.   6. The Himalayan Glade in September: the scarlet fruits of *Cotoneaster horizontalis* contrast with the soft pink of *Polygonum vacciniifolium* which covers the sandstone bluffs.   7. Tony Schilling's soft-colour plantings in the walled Henry Price Garden at Wakehurst Place include *Penstemon* 'Evelyn', *Spiraea japonica* 'Walluf' and *Erysimum* 'Bowles Mauve'.

32

6.

7.

Threave Gardens and School of Gardening, Castle Douglas, Dumfries and Galloway

BILL HEAN

A property of the National Trust for Scotland, Threave is on the A75 a mile west of Castle Douglas. It differs from other Trust gardens in that it was not historically important or noteworthy, nor did it complement a fine building. The property was accepted by the Trust in 1948 because it constituted a complete estate with a good integration of farming, forestry and wildlife. The house, *circa* 1870, was sound but uninteresting, situated in a parkland setting surrounded by groups of hardwoods, while the garden consisted of a one-acre walled garden of traditional design, with some elderly lean-to glasshouses. One redeeming feature was a large, if vintage, collection of daffodils, which were planted throughout the woods and were the only horticultural interest of the previous owner and donor, Major Alan Gordon, DSO, MC.

The Trust's initial problem was to find a use for the house and the garden, and this was neatly solved by the creation in 1960 of the Threave School of Gardening, with the object of training young people to be professional practical gardeners; Threave House was to be used as a hostel and the sixty-five acres surrounding it were designated for garden development.

Having been appointed to the post of Principal at the outset I have had the enjoyment of being involved in the gradual development of the garden over twenty-five years, most of which time I have had as my deputy Magnus Ramsay, who has played a major part in the design and construction and is responsible for organizing all the day-to-day work which keeps the flesh on the bones of a garden.

From the outset Threave was designed as a teaching garden, an outdoor classroom, using the sixty-plus acres of grassland and the groups of trees which surrounded Threave House. Whereas in most National Trust gardens the question is always 'What would the owner or the designer have done here?' we at Threave were released from such inhibitions and were able to design and plant as we felt fitted the need. Twenty-five years may seem a long time to develop sixty-five acres fully, but this is a garden which will never be complete; already whole sections have been ripped out and redesigned when the need arose for a student design project. Having previously looked after the arboretum department at Edinburgh Botanic Gardens, where woody plants were retained for scientific reasons long after their ornamental value had gone, and then come to Threave where we were starting from scratch with young plants, I have come to the conclusion that most gardeners keep woody plants far too long. There are always exceptions where the venerable specimen flowers, fruits and seeds better, but in many cases it is the younger plant which gives the superior show – and occupies less space in the process.

Every gardener has to work within the constraints of the climate, soil, aspect and contours of his or her patch, and at Threave the plusses just about cancel out the minus factors; 50 inches (125cm) of rain with a heavy, silty soil means you don't suffer from drought and never have to water – but you can lose a lot of plants from wet feet and it is better to leave the soil strictly alone from December to March.

The garden is on the side of a hill with aspects ranging from south-west to north-west; it is a difficult place to shelter and one must accept that there are areas which will always be windy and plan accordingly. The open situation also gets most light and this suits the heathers, conifers and, less obviously, the eucalyptus, which survive in the openest and windiest place whereas those in shelter succumb to frost. But the main advantage of having a garden on a hill is the views; from Threave we can look across to the Galloway Hills on a clear day, with Merrick, at just under 3,000 ft the highest point in the south of Scotland, showing up nearly forty miles away.

Rock, either outcropping or just below the surface, is common in south-west Scotland, and can result in plants being stunted if it is not realized just how close to the surface the rock lies.

Although Threave is situated in the south-west corner of Scotland we gain little from the moderating influence of the Gulf Stream, while gardens such as Logan Botanic Garden, on the coast fifty miles to the west of us, are on a par climatically with Cornwall and the Scillies.

Being principally a teaching establishment, the design incorporates as many types of garden and as wide a range of plants as possible. We have never gone for the rare or difficult plant, inclining always to plants which we think will do well with us and which have a good garden value. We try to undertake one major project each winter; this can often begin with a design class, followed by laying out, preparing and planting, the whole job being seen

. Bill Hean.

through by one group of students. In this way the garden has grown over the years.

We first rebuilt the glass, formed a nursery and propagation unit and established a fruit and vegetable garden. At no time did we buy in large numbers of plants: we do our own propagation from stock plants or from cuttings and seeds given by friends; we often start an area with a fairly simple design and add new beds gradually as stock becomes available.

The two elements most seriously lacking on the rolling grassy landscape in the early days were water features and hard landscaping, and these we have tried to incorporate whenever the opportunity and a suitable site presented itself. We now have two ponds in the garden, one with a cascade fed by a supply pumped from the pool, the other a larger pond fed from the land drains. A patio, several garden shelters and a sunken garden give a more permanent look to the place, as only stonework can.

The first development was in the area around the walled garden and consisted of a peat garden, an ideal use for a shady north-facing plot; twenty-five years and several replantings later this is the home of a good collection of dwarf ericaceous shrubs, primulas and meconopsis. It is one of my favourite areas in April and May, when it is a riot of colour if the late frosts don't finish it off.

The rock garden started life as a series of rocky outcrops or 'knowes' as they are known in Galloway; by stripping off some turf and clearing a bit of soil, we revealed the bones of a rock garden, to which over the years we have added many loads of rock, always looking for more height to give better drainage, the main problem of rock gardeners on a wet, silty soil. This was followed in succeeding years by a woodland garden in an already established copse of about an acre, and above that a rose garden. The order of development was always a geographical one, working outwards from a central point and, as we came to each area, deciding which group of plants it was best suited for. Level ground being almost non-existent,

formal features are difficult to fit in, hence the largely informal nature of the garden.

The terrace round the house gives us a chance to do a little formal spring and summer bedding, and below the terrace we have a good selection of informal herbaceous beds; we avoid staking simply by selecting plants which are of small to medium height or resilient enough to support themselves in an exposed site.

Close by, a heath garden constructed in 1963 made a fine contribution to the scene; we used as framework planting semi-mature birches and rowans lifted from woods around the estate. Heathers, I feel, reach their peak five to ten years after planting and thereafter they tend to deteriorate. After eighteen years replanting of some areas became necessary but one never gets the same vigorous growth the second time round so the collection was re-established using young plants on a new site and is now looking splendid.

By 1982 the old heath garden site was ready for redevelopment and, by fencing the area in and creating a garden within a garden, we were able to reduce the scale and include many features which we couldn't otherwise have done. This area is now a secret garden, completely enclosed, with only one entrance through a laburnum arch. The trellis makes a good site for clematis and loniceras; the theme of this garden is foliage plants, ranging from grasses and sedges through bolder herbaceous plants such as acanthus to good trees and shrubs like the golden Scots pine – a survivor of the heath garden – and *Aralia elata* 'Variegata'. In this area we have let imagination run riot and included such features as dry river beds, a sunken garden, bridges and garden ornaments.

One other area worthy of mention is the dwarf conifer collection. The idea was inspired by a visit paid to the National Arboretum in Washington, DC, in 1969 where I saw the magnificent Gotelli collection of conifers. Prior to this we had used these plants to

35

complement rock gardens or heather beds but there is no doubt they are at their best as a collection. The soil on our conifer beds is covered with 500g black polythene and topped with a good inch (30mm) of gravel, which eliminates weeding and allows visitors to walk on the beds to examine the plants.

The remainder of the garden is taken up by trees and shrubs and already, after twenty years, we are removing more than we are planting. We all tend to plant too closely but no harm and often a lot of good is done by it, as long as one is strong minded enough to remove healthy young plants when necessary.

Making a garden involves much hard work, but to my mind it is the most enjoyable part of the job and while we have a garden we should never be finished improving.

2. The heather garden above Threave faces south to the hills of Cairnsmoor of Fleet; here a lone Austrian pine stands above a planting of *Erica × darleyensis*. 3. Below the house, herbaceous beds set in the hillside lawns contain abundant plantings of *Campanula lactiflora*, setting off others like hemerocallis, phlox and delphiniums. 4. The rock garden is mostly natural rock outcrop. Here, looking north to the Galloway Hills, the small-flowered red *Dianthus deltoides* spreads alongside the yellow *Genista tinctoria* 'Plena'.

2.

3.

4

5. A purple and cream bearded iris planted imaginatively with *Polygonum bistorta* 'Superbum'. 6. The walled garden is set in the old kitchen garden; *Lilium regale* and *Lilium* 'Enchantment' make a fine show. 7. The daffodil bank sweeps down from Threave House with a superb display of the white *Narcissus* 'Southern Gem'.

6.

7.

Savill Garden and the Valley Gardens, Windsor, Berkshire

JOHN BOND, VMH

When I was just sixteen, I had already gained good experience working in a Cotswold tree and shrub nursery which had become somewhat run down due to the restrictions caused by the war. I then went to Bodnant as an improver, in answer to an advertisement in *The Gardeners' Chronicle*. This presented a unique opportunity, and I approached my new job with some trepidation and great excitement. I believe that the three years spent in this great garden were the most important (horticulturally) of my life and have much for which to thank Charles Puddle (the recently retired Head Gardener) and Bodnant in general.

I was then employed by Hilliers of Winchester as a propagator and for four years I was involved in the production of a very wide range of calcifuge trees

1. John Bond in the Dry Garden.

and shrubs. Promotion came my way, and at twenty-six I found myself responsible for 150 acres of nursery and a staff of forty. It was my task to grow all Hilliers' rhododendrons, conifers, magnolias, camellias, Japanese maples and much more. I was also responsible for the very first plantings in the now world-famous Hillier Arboretum which adjoined my 'patch'. This was a wonderful period for me, for the fifties were the heyday of Hilliers as a plantsman's nursery and so much of my plant knowledge was obtained there.

Whilst nursery stock production is interesting, most plants leave the care of the grower long before they mature, and as the son and grandson of Head Gardeners I had a yearning to be involved in a great garden where a range of plants of variable age and size were grown.

And so my story progresses. In 1962, after my first meeting with Sir Eric Savill and a fairly gruelling interview, I was offered the post of Assistant Keeper of the Gardens in Windsor Great Park. I was promoted to Joint Keeper of the Gardens in 1970 with responsibility for the Valley Gardens, the propagation department and the students. In 1974 I was appointed Keeper of the Gardens, with total control of the department. A further garden, Frogmore, was added to my responsibilities in 1977.

In 1932 Eric Savill, a new surveyor (soon to be appointed Deputy Ranger), came to the Crown Estate at Windsor. The estate offered great scope for improvement and further development and Eric Savill, an exceptionally forceful person, soon began to make changes

– the farmed areas were transformed and extended, the forestry grew by leaps and bounds, and numerous estate houses of a very high standard were built for the considerably increased numbers of staff. The fine landscaped park had been developed in Georgian times, but gardens of any description were completely lacking. Having looked at several areas, Eric Savill settled upon an area adjoining a small estate tree nursery – Parkside Nursery – which offered a variety of terrain and conditions within the limitations of the Berkshire–Surrey heathland. There were ample wet boggy areas (the garden was soon christened The Bog Garden by local people) and a fairly lively watercourse. This stream was developed and two sizeable ponds were made. Drier woodland was also available with some excellent oak, sweet chestnut and beech providing a canopy for rhododendrons, etc. In addition, the well-cultivated soil of the nursery, which was soon closed, was well suited to the needs of roses and herbaceous border plants, and this area is now almost exactly covered by our rather more formal summer garden.

A few years of steady development went by before King George V and Queen Mary made their first visit. Eric Savill used Queen Mary's comment, 'It's very small, Mr Savill, do get on with it,' as his green light. It was, however, King George VI and Queen Elizabeth The Queen Mother who gave him the greatest encouragement. As the Duke and Duchess of York, they were developing the garden at the nearby Royal Lodge on much the same lines, and a very happy association was built up with exchanges of ideas, plants and

2. The moss in the Beech Wood at the Savill Garden.

labour. This happy link continued until the outbreak of the 1939–45 war. Queen Elizabeth The Queen Mother's support to this day is very much valued, and she frequently makes private visits to the Savill Garden without prior announcement. She is particularly interested in the contents of the Temperate House, the tender rhododendrons with their very fine scent being her great favourites.

The war inevitably brought development to a halt, with only a couple of ladies keeping the bracken and brambles at bay. By 1949, life and work having returned to normal, the thirty-five-acre garden was completed and was already

being hailed as one of the leading woodland gardens of the temperate world.

Eric Savill was knighted by Her Majesty The Queen in 1953; he also received many awards from the Royal Horticultural Society, including the Victoria Medal of Honour. It was, however, King George VI's decision to name the garden the Savill Garden which gave him the greatest pleasure, and which he considered his greatest honour.

Having completed the Savill Garden, Eric Savill set his sights on the attractive area of land on the north bank of Virginia Water. The work of clearing and development began in 1949 and by 1960

some 300 acres had been planted, which included the Valley Garden, a superb mixed woodland planting of the finest rhododendrons (both species and hybrids), camellias, magnolias and countless other suitable plants. The much-visited and photographed Azalea Punch Bowl is also in this area. The foundation of the second area was the Rhododendron Species Collection, which had been gathered together over a period of forty years or so at Tower Court, Ascot, by the late J. B. Stevenson; it was purchased from his widow and transferred to the Great Park by estate staff between 1951 and 1953. This area of approximately fifty acres is the largest collection of rhododendron species in cultivation; whilst rhododendron hybrids are, of course, banned, a wide range of appropriate trees, shrubs and herbaceous plants are used in a supporting role. The third area to be developed, again from 1951, was a ten-acre Heather Garden on the site of a shallow gravel pit, which had last been worked prior to the 1914–18 war. This area added a considerable amount of new interest to the Valley Gardens, which are mostly woodland, for here we have an open area where many sun-loving shrubs are grown in addition to the heathers. These three areas, contrasting in their appearance and aims, join together to make the Valley Gardens.

There is no doubt that Eric Savill's horticultural achievements were unique and I am forever conscious of the responsibility and the challenge as I follow in his footsteps.

What, then, are my policies concerning the management of these great gardens? First, I am determined to maintain what I have inherited to a very high standard and whilst routine weeding, grass cutting, watering and mulching (mulching, incidentally, is my second religion) are vital, there is another aspect of maintenance which is of even greater importance. The woodland areas are examined critically every five years or so, and trees and shrubs are pruned, transplanted if necessary and possible, and removed if inferior or

39

3.

4.

5.

3. A June morning in the Savill's Bog Garden with *Primula japonica* and *P. helodoxa* interspersed with blue meconopsis: the fern is *Matteuccia struthiopteris*.   4. Nearly every available space in the Temperate House is filled including, high up, the yellow *Acacia linearifolia*. Lower down, the tree fern *Dicksonia antarctica* grows behind *Camellia reticulata* 'Willow Wand' and white *Rhododenron cubittii*.   5. The Azalea Valley in the Valley Gardens, brilliant with Knaphill and Ghent rhododendron hybrids.   6. Early April at the Savill Garden has the sculptural shapes of golden yellow *Lysichitum americanum* and white *Lysichitum camtschatcense* set against the long drifts of *Narcissus bulbocodium* 'Citrinus'.

tiring. Herbaceous material is also divided and, where space allows, new subjects are added, thus maintaining a balance of young and mature plants. This policy also ensures that the garden does not stand still, for a static garden is a dead garden which rapidly goes into decline. The woodland garden is very much a spring garden, but great thought and care are taken to plant subjects which have more than one season of interest, and the summer, autumn and winter periods are rapidly gaining strength.

Secondly, we are going forward with a programme of sensible steady expansion. Woodland gardening allows this, unlike formal gardening which is always labour intensive, for if new plantings are made thoughtfully, with the aid of ample mulch, they soon create ground cover and lessen the need for weeding. The dome shapes of the dwarfer and middle-sized rhododendrons and hydrangeas and the low complete cover of evergreen azaleas and hostas are good examples of this. We rarely have the opportunity to make a development as different and exciting as the new Dry Garden in the Savill Garden. The site was cleared in 1977. The idea came to me during the frightening drought of 1976, and the first plantings

6.

our part, have gathered together some smaller groups and we have a complete collection of our own hybrids, almost all of the magnificent loderi hybrids, a large and growing range of the older hardy hybrids and a very great number of North American bred hybrids. Loosely connected with this work is the need to grow the great wealth of new material, both wild and selected by man, on an unofficial trial basis to ascertain its value in British gardens. Many of these, such as magnolias, hollies and the new American rhododendron hybrids mentioned above are included in our collections.

If we are to keep our great gardens 'alive', sensible changes must be accepted. The need to produce income is an example of this; in recent years we have adapted our propagation unit and created two new units where we now grow a wide range of containerized plants, mainly in the more unusual category, although some 'bread and butter' is produced. As before, our own needs come first, for we use considerable quantities of plants here in the gardens. The surplus is then offered to the trade – we issue two lists annually, and sell to the public through our very successful plant shop at the entrance to the Savill Garden. Apart from the income this produces, I gain a good deal of satisfaction from distributing good, new and unusual plants, many of them not obtainable elsewhere.

The notes above are just part of my task and the task of my very skilled and conscientious staff, for I would not want to give the impression that I operate a one-man band. It is a monumental task and not a nine-to-five job; it is usually a fourteen-hour day, frequently seven days a week, but it is rewarding. Apart from my love of plants, the great reward is to work for the thousands of people who visit the gardens annually. One last reward – the award by the Royal Horticultural Society of the Victoria Medal of Honour in Horticulture in 1981 was clearly the greatest award any gardener could receive; a great award, indeed.

were made in 1978. No attempt was made to reproduce a piece of mountainside or desert; we have simply created conditions for dry-soil shrubs and plants from any area of the world – obviously subjects from California, the Mediterranean region, South Africa and Australasia are much to the fore. This wide range of plants provides colour and interest from early spring, with the advent of the pulsatillas, until October, when the zauschnerias are still presenting themselves well.

Thirdly, our National Collections will be developed further, for I am fully committed to doing my best to ensure that we preserve/conserve as wide a range as possible of the genera which flourish in our conditions. During the past five years we have been made responsible for five National Collections – Rhododendron Species (the original Tower Court collection has been and is being added to at a fair rate), Magnolias, Dwarf and Slow-growing Conifers (a mammoth task, the world appears to be full of them), Hollies and the Glenn Dale Azaleas. Other groups which are being carefully gathered together and indexed are astilbes, hostas, Japanese maples and maples in general, pieris and hydrangeas. Rhododendron hybrids in general present a vast task and no one garden can tackle them alone. We, for

2 Dalebrook, Gorsley, Ross-on-Wye, Herefordshire

ERIC PYMONT

We decided to move out of the town in 1973 when our youngest child was about to leave school; our major consideration in choosing where to live was the size of the garden. Fortune smiled upon us and we were extremely lucky to find a site with a new bungalow under construction and some extra land for sale. An area of nearly two acres, it was a gardener's dream in that it had a stream running through, albeit culverted for much of its length. At least there was water present – just how much, we have discovered since at the annual flood time.

As a professional horticulturalist I had been accustomed to large areas, and had felt rather cramped and frustrated in a small town plot. This was our chance. There are so many plants we would like to grow, but at the same time I see nothing attractive in some bedraggled and obviously unhappy specimen grown purely for its rarity value. Our plants have to pay their rent. Our two conflicting interests, then, are a desire to collect plants for their own sake and an attempt to have a garden which is attractive as a whole. It is not always easy to reconcile these two viewpoints: how successful we have been must be decided by the visitor.

The garden was planned in advance, as there was an interval of seven months between initial purchase and occupation. My goodness, how we planned! Great fun – but in the event the garden still largely evolved over a period of years, and in only one or two aspects have we followed the original plan, notably in the small rock garden at the east end of the bungalow, so obviously demanded on the steep slope.

Our first plans were frustrated by the great depth of clay and stones, a legacy of the builders, which we found immediately around the house. We had brought many plants with us in the June move which needed a home immediately, and the compacted clay soil where we had intended to have a flowerbed would have taken a long time in preparation, so an alternative site was chosen for the first flower-bed, where soil conditions were better.

The garden, as one would assume from the presence of the stream, is at the bottom of a valley. Annual flooding has left a depth of some four feet of good soil in the bottom, a light silty loam, the best garden soil that I have ever been privileged to handle. This, coupled with the fact that the bottom of the garden never dries out completely (not even in 1976), must be responsible for the magnificent growth shown by most of our plants.

This growth has surprised me and has brought home with a thud the fact that a gardener can never stop learning. When we came to Gorsley I had been in horticulture for thirty years, less five for war service, and had begun to think that I knew a thing or two. This plot has furthered my horticultural education, but I will not say it completed it. Plants – for example some heleniums and heliopsis – which grew to three feet in our previous garden reach six feet in this one and have had to be replaced with less vigorous varieties.

Curiously, although wet, the soil seems free-draining. I cannot entirely explain this apparent paradox. It has been a great eye-opener to me that many ordinary garden plants which we do not normally consider to be bog plants will tolerate these wet conditions.

The advice I give to those moving to a new garden is, 'Do nothing for the first year, evaluate the site thoroughly in all winds and weathers, and then plan accordingly.' But of course I do not follow this excellent advice myself – I am far too anxious to make a start. We therefore planted what we had or could acquire, a normal range of garden plants, regardless of the moisture – indeed partly in ignorance, because we happened to have two winters rather drier than average at this time and we were not aware of how wet the garden would be. Phlox, as one would expect, appreciate the moisture, but even delphiniums, stokesias, pyrethrums and many other herbaceous species and

1. Eric Pymont tying *Pyrus salicifolia*.

2. The pool, with erica beds beyond.

3. The view from the pool towards the Solardome greenhouse includes the rock garden on the right.

cultivars thrive on it. It is our policy to try everything, and few plants have needed a move to a drier site. This is just as well, as our drier areas are extremely limited.

We have been doubly fortunate in that our ground is full of the small wild daffodil, *Narcissus pseudonarcissus*, for which this district is renowned. We could see in the first spring before moving in that there were some present, but we were very pleasantly surprised the next year to find so many. The ground occupied by these is mowed only when the seed is ripening, so they have had plenty of chance to spread, and this care has been amply rewarded by the subsequent increase. We estimate that they take about four years to flower from seed. We are now reaching saturation

4. Eric Pymont's swamp garden is home mainly for primulas (*P. japonica* and *P. helodoxa*), but here also are variegated carex, *Iris pseudacorus* Variegata and *Gunnera manicata*.   5. Eric Pymont's raised bed, topped by a hedge of lavender, contains dwarf conifers and alpines and bulbs requiring sharper drainage and drier conditions.   6. Island beds in the garden are filled with perennials: kniphofia, *Astrantia major* (white), *Phlox paniculata* (pink), *Lychnis chalcedonica* (scarlet) and *Achillea* 'Gold Plate' are in the near bed and, beyond, campanulas and more phlox in front of the light-leaved tree, *Aralia elata* 'Aureomarginata'.   7. The wild daffodil, *Narcissus pseudonarcissus*, is common locally and Eric has encouraged them to spread. He thinks they have now reached saturation point!   8. *Hosta fortunei* 'Aureomarginata' forms the fresh foreground to this view of the pool; beyond are *Primula florindae*, vincas, golden philadelphus and white astilbes.

5.

6.

point. The stage can be reached, I believe, when there are too many. I would sooner see irregular drifts of varying densities than just one solid block of colour. The problem will probably solve itself, as this year, following several requests, we have gathered over one pound of daffodil seed for friends in various parts of the country. Another seed we have been able to distribute is that of the cowslip, *Primula veris*.

While the bottom of our tiny valley is accumulated soil, the sloping bank consists of about three inches of soil over shale, very well drained, but with a fair supply of water seeping down from higher levels. We therefore have two quite different habitats. This grassy bank is also colonized by the wild daffodil. It is interesting to note its ability to colonize both these areas and the local woodland as well. Once the daffodil seed is ripe the grass can be cut, and it is cut fairly close for the rest of the year, fortnightly or thereabouts, it being our aim to kill out the more vigorous grasses, docks and nettles. In this we have been successful and there has been a wonderful bonus in the wild flowers which have grown along this bank. Few were apparent in the first year – evidently they had been suppressed by the rank growth of grasses and docks. Cowslips were the first to appear in numbers, and these have spread through the garden, even becoming a nuisance in some beds.

In addition there are now on this bank violets, wood anemones, birdsfoot trefoil, ladies' bedstraw, hard heads, early purple and spotted orchids, buttercups and many others. The flowers provide interest from March to late June and the bank is now cut later than the lower-lying daffodil ground. There is a final fling in the autumn with the wild colchicums. Pale purple and very fragile, they are gradually spreading but are not as reliable in their flowering as most of the other wildlings. This bank creates a lot of interest amongst visitors, bringing back memories of the English meadows of the past.

We like to have some colour in due season and the phloxes are probably the best providers, but flowers are short-lived, whereas foliage is so much longer-lasting. We have aimed therefore at foliage effects as much as anything. Our greys are limited by the wetness, but hostas thrive and they alone provide some wonderful effects. Many of our most telling associations have come about by accident, but we are always prepared to move plants if the appearance can be improved.

Never being satisfied, we managed to acquire a further piece of land after some years by renting it from a neighbour. Shown as a pond by the Ordinance Survey, it had been fenced off to keep his cattle out. We have dug channels in it to make a water garden, where we grow bog primulas. These are gradually spreading around the garden, the seed presumably being carried by flood-water.

Other plants too we allow to seed around. For instance, the variegated honesty, purple orache (*Atriplex*), rose plantain, purple plantain and Scotch thistle (*Onopordon acanthium*). Numbers can be reduced if they become too invasive. The policy of allowing seedlings to grow willy-nilly means that weed control has to be done largely by hand. In fact the ground is too wet for hoeing in most seasons except in the small vegetable plot, which is re-dug annually. We therefore spend much time upon our knees engaged in hand weeding.

A large number of variegated plants grow in our garden; we like them and we are always seeking more. We have planted many trees and have been extremely gratified by the amount of growth they have made. In ten years they now really have a presence in the garden and begin to create the desired effect.

When we moved in, the whole plot was bare apart from one or two trees on the periphery. Everything was open. We have attempted to create some hidden corners so that there is an element of surprise in parts of the garden.

The amount of interest shown in this garden has amazed us. Friends of course came to see it. Those who were active in their local gardening societies then brought a party from the society, and so the word spread around. Gardeners are a generous crowd and we readily acknowledge the help we have received in gifts of plants from many sources. Our garden gives us endless pleasure. If we can share it with others and at the same time raise some money for charity we are only too pleased to do so.

7.

8.

Abbotswood, Stow-on-the-Wold, Gloucestershire

DENNIS SMALLEY

The Cotswolds form one of the most beautiful parts of England – hilly, sheep-grazing country. Abbotswood was bought by Mr Robin Sculley in 1970 and he engaged me as head gardener at the same time, his main instruction being to keep the garden as near to the original Gertrude Jekyll plan as possible.

Sir Edwin Lutyens, who was commissioned by Mark Fenwick in the early part of this century to extend the house, worked with Miss Jekyll on the garden design. On settling down with her books, it was not long before I discovered that the main point about her work was her thoughtful use of colour.

She was originally an artist and particularly enjoyed water-colour painting. This can be seen in much of her

work, the colour starting off in the pale blues, moving off into whites and yellows and then to oranges, crimsons and reds, the scheme then going back through the cooler whites and yellows into lavender blues and silvers. She understood that one of the secrets of the successful use of colour lay in the relationship with the colours around it; for instance, she suggested putting the complementary colour of yellow into a blue garden, thus enhancing the blue.

All the same, Miss Jekyll did not neglect any colour because it was too brilliant; she realized that all colours have a value if thoughtfully used. This thinking extended beyond flowers to that of foliage colour and the countless shades of green. She also combined different textures and plant

forms for their pictorial effect.

The entrance and approach to Abbotswood is informal compared with the garden beyond the house. It starts with a long, Cotswold drystone wall which runs along the length of the road from Stow-on-the-Wold; from the gates the long drive winds through groups of trees and shrubs planted in Mr Fenwick's time. One of the features of this part of the garden is the planting of rhododendrons and azaleas, unexpected here on limestone. Mark Fenwick arranged for whole wagons full of sandy loam to be transported from Somerset to Moreton in Marsh railway station; from there, teams of horses hauled the soil to Abbotswood.

On the left-hand side of the drive is a long hill and a stream meanders through the rhododendrons and azaleas and disappears into thicker woodland beyond the formal terraces on the other side of the drive. Great stands of *Cercidiphyllum japonicum* also flourish here, giving a wonderful colour in the autumn, often being the first to change. On the same bank in spring are masses of fritillaries (the snakeshead *Fritillaria meleagris*) and a blue carpet of scillas.

The stream, which is planted with various species of primulas and the occasional clump of *Rheum palmatum*, comes into its own just below the drive where it is dammed into a series of pools. The dams provide bridges to look down on to the surface of the water and into the depths below. The top pool is surrounded by statuesque moisture-lovers such as *Rodgersia tabularis*, a small version of *Gunnera manicata*, ligularias and lysichitons.

On the south side of the house is a

1. Dennis Smalley.

mall rectangular canal, flanked by two high stone walls – the Tank Garden. Its most imposing feature is a wide archway in the shape of a scallop shell set into the house. Above the shell a stone river-god spouts water into the pool below and this contains tubs of irises ('Naomi', 'Sumptosa', 'James Brydon' and 'Opal'), surrounded by water lilies. The irises were divided up about three years ago and, as a result, some flowered which have never done so before. Now we have varying heights and flowering seasons in each tub.

Around the corner, the two formal terraces lead spectacularly down, one below the other; seen from the house, they are backed by the contrasting landscape of the fields and hills beyond. It would be fair to say that the terraces correspond in spirit to the original Jekyll planting but not in every detail. The first terrace reaches out for about sixty feet and contains, on either side of the centre garden of variously shaped herbaceous and annual beds, two long, narrow parterre gardens, one containing roses, intricately patterned with low box hedges. These are separated from the centre garden by yew hedges.

This elaborate terrace is in strong contrast to the lower one which is linked to it by steps in the centre of a stone retaining wall about eight feet high. In this open part of the garden the planting is confined to six-foot-wide outer borders; in the middle of the lawn is a narrow rectangular canal planted with irises with a statue in the middle. In one corner of this garden an octagonal, stone-built gazebo overlooks the borders, its timbers weathered to a pleasant silver-grey. The planting here is mainly herbaceous and in need of some division to reduce the well-established clumps, in particular the thalictrums and erigerons. A fine pair of ornamental gates in the lower wall links the garden romantically to the sheep pastures in the Stow countryside.

Gertrude Jekyll designed a rose pergola to run from the north side of the house down past both terraces. This was dismantled by a former owner as part of

2. The Tank Garden.

a plan, after the last war (during which there was only one gardener here), to reduce the maintenance in the garden. Some of the original photographs show the pergola with huge Ali Baba pots standing between each brick support. It looked very good and complemented the scheme for this part of the garden. To the north of the house are the Heather and Alpine Gardens. Both were badly neglected during the last war, but we now have plans to restore this area.

The formal gardens are kept as much as possible to the original planting.

Sadly, over the last few years we have lost a great many trees and plants with the extreme weather we have here.

Much replanting has been done, but there is always more to do. I like to introduce something different into the garden, wherever possible. Bringing the woodland gradually into the garden has been very interesting and rewarding for my young gardeners. I like to train my own staff and employ boys from local schools.

Abbotswood is opened to the public four Sundays in April and May for charity.

3.

4.

5.

3. The Lutyens-designed canal in the lower garden is planted with water lilies and tubs of *Iris* 'Naomi': on the far wall is the grape vine *Vitis vinifera* 'Brandt'.

4. The Rose Garden, which includes 'Iceberg', 'Mischief' and 'Dainty Maid', is set in an ingenious series of geometrical parterres.

5. Gertrude Jekyll was interested in the effects of self-seeding, as here on the Rock Bank where aquilegia and Iceland poppies grow profusely.

6.

7.   8.

6. The centre formal garden, *Cotinus coggygria* in the foreground, with *Antirrhinum* 'Nelrose' and *Stachys lanata* in the round bed, effectively 'borrows' the Cotswold landscape, with Stow church on the hill.   7. The West Wall Border at hay harvest is soft with the pinks of pyrethrums, sweet williams, stocks, roses and, in the wall, heuchera.   8. Spring on the Stream Garden Bank includes *Rhododendron* 'Pink Pearl', *Acer palmatum* 'Dissectum Atropurpureum' and the azalea 'Kirin', growing informally with buttercups and scillas.

Sheffield Park Garden, Uckfield, Sussex

ARCHIE SKINNER

My interest in plants came long before an interest in gardens or gardening. I cannot remember a time when I was not enthralled by flowers. The first to make an impression, a still longed-for joy each season, was the wild dog rose; even as a small boy I thought its transient beauty something to be savoured.

The few roses in my parents' garden were also enjoyed: 'Charles Mallerin', the darkest of reds, 'Betty Uprichard', a nice pink, 'Lady Sylvia', shell pink, loved by everyone, and then, a little later, the rose of the century, 'Peace'. The garden always had rosemary for remembrance and a lavender; both grew well in the climate of the English Riviera in Devon. This love of plants is as strong as ever, but is now combined with a love of gardens and gardening.

1. Archie Skinner on the bridge of the Stream Garden.

Every head gardener would, I am sure, pay tribute to the previous generation of gardeners who have influenced them, men who have willingly passed on their experience and skills. Their love of plants was infectious; our achievements, if any, are due to their encouragement and help.

I was fortunate that my arrival at Sheffield Park fourteen years ago coincided with a need to carry out some reclamation of quite large areas, to cope with the ever-increasing numbers of visitors. Much has been achieved in that time, with a willing, enthusiastic and hard-working staff.

The first project was the opening up of the Palm Walk glade. A mass of bamboo, Portuguese laurel, seedling birch and bramble was cleared, to reveal an avenue of palms, *Trachycarpus fortunei*. We also found such good things as *Rhododendron barbatum*, *R. yunnanense*, *Umbellularia californica* and *Pieris floribunda*. To provide colour in August in this area large beds of hydrangeas have been planted, with an emphasis on the lacecap types, which, we think, fit in with the natural setting: *H.* 'Grayswood', 'Rosealba', 'Veitchii', 'Blue Wave' and 'Lanarth White'.

Another major project was undertaken in 1976–7, when it was decided to develop a large area to the east of the third lake, to be called the Queen's Walk to commemorate the jubilee of Her Majesty the Queen. This has given particular pleasure, as it has enabled us to make a contribution to the conservation of our native flora. We have been able to keep what was once the cricket field (Australian cricket teams played here in the late 1800s) as an area of interest to botanists and conservationists, by allowing the wild flowers to seed and disperse before cutting the grass. These include many thousands of spotted orchids, *Dactylorhiza maculata*. The area is now of sufficient interest for the Sussex Botanical Recording Society to carry out yearly surveys. In 1983, no less than 169 species were recorded. Butterflies too have benefited greatly from what is now an old-fashioned English meadow.

Between this meadow and the third lake is the walk itself, meandering around the lake, with a steep bank on one side. Evergreen azaleas are being planted, not only to provide colour in the years to come, but also to reduce maintenance when they have grown together to form thick ground cover. Cultivars already growing well are 'Hinomayo', a clear soft pink, 'Beethoven', a mauve-pink, 'Suga-no-ito', a pale lavender-pink, *Rhododendron kiusianum*, in mixed colours, and 'Mother's Day', a red. Camellias – 'Donation', 'Nobilissima', 'Inspiration', and *Camellia cuspidata* – we have found, do very well on this bank in the dappled shade facing north-west, no doubt responding to an annual mulch of well-rotted leaf mould.

The Stream Garden is another area which gives me particular pleasure. To the south of the gentian beds was an area of about three or four acres, containing some very nice conifers, such as *Pinus pinaster*, *Abies procera*, *Picea likiangensis*, *Cephalotaxus fortunei*, and also a mass of bramble and bracken, seedling sycamores and fallen trees.

During clearance we found an old drainage ditch. Over the past four years (it is a winter job), we have widened it and cleaned it out, and put in dams so that we could hear the noise of water dropping to the lower levels. Having no stone or rock to make the dams we used wood – sweet chestnut, made watertight with blue clay purchased from the local brickworks. (We always have a supply for the repairing of any leaks which occur in our lakes.)

The margins of the stream are being planted with moisture-loving perennials, among them a wide variety of hostas, including the elegant 'Tallboy', *H. fortunei* and *H. fortunei* 'Aurea'. The arum lily 'Crowborough' is thriving in the water at the edge of the stream, providing an exotic touch when in flower.

No stream garden would be complete without a group of candelabra primulas, those lovely natives of China and Japan. A large bed contains *Primula pulverulenta*, one of the easiest, its mauve tiers of flowers borne on distinctive mealy stems. *P. bulleyana* produces healthy clumps from which arise whorls of orange-yellow flowers. Not in the candelabra section, but perhaps better known in smaller gardens, is *P. denticulata*, the drumstick primula – their rigid stems are topped by a tight round head of flowers in varying shades of blue, white, pink and red. Our original, from which we worked up a stock, came from my sister's garden. It is a pleasing lavender-blue. They are rather stiff, perhaps a little too formal in the woodland garden, especially in large groups, but dispersed and scattered, as if by wind-blown seed, they are acceptable.

Many of the old varieties of *Iris sibirica* are becoming scarce, so we have been trying to conserve them and some of them will eventually be planted in the stream garden. I am very fond of *Leucojum aestivum*, the summer snowflake – in spite of its common name, it blooms in May. This British native, which prefers moist situations, is planted in a bed beside the stream and interplanted with ferns, so the bed has an agreeable covering when the leuco-

2. Climbing rose 'Cécile Brunner' and *Abutilon vitifolium* decorate Archie Skinner's home.

jums are past their best. The same ploy has been used to give shade to the bulbs of the imposing giant lily of the Himalayas, *Cardiocrinum giganteum*, of which we have just a few. We hope they will do well, as they have had VIP treatment – a bed containing a rich fare of well-rotted manure and leafmould.

Not a single plant in our stream garden has been purchased. All have been given, sometimes only a single plant, and stock has been worked up by division: for example, *Hosta* 'Honeybells' came from Mr Graham Thomas, *Primula pulverulenta* from Mr Alan Hardy of Sandling Park and the cardiocrinum from Mr Tony Schilling.

There has been an involvement with the NCCPG – the National Council for the Conservation of Plants and Gardens. My personal interest is in the

saving of the old Ghent azaleas, which were once popular garden plants but are now sadly scarce and in need of conservation. I first started to collect them about six years ago, after a conversation over coffee at one of the Royal Horticultural Society shows with several other gardeners who were concerned that so many good plants were being neglected. The Ghent azaleas were first bred by a Belgian baker in the 1820s and 1830s. He hybridized the newly introduced *Rhododendron nudiflorum viscosum* and *R. calendulaceum* of North America with the lovely, sweetly scented *R. luteum*. Ghent azaleas went out of favour when the Knaphill and Exbury hybrids came to the fore in the 1920s and 1930s. This was a great pity because the Ghents do have charm – their long funnel-shaped flowers with

3. The Stream Garden, a pet project of Archie Skinner's. Along with ferns and hostas, the blue *Iris sibirica*, *I.s.* 'Wisley White' and meconopsis flourish here in June.

protruding stamens are scented and are borne in late May and early June, when most other rhododendrons have finished flowering. They also contribute to the autumnal scene, with their bright hues of red and russet foliage. The collection of some twenty-three cultivars is now the National Collection, which we hope will be increased as more come to light.

Rhododendron sargentianum, which came with me from Devon when I came to Sheffield Park, is too small for the landscaped garden, but very much 'at home' in our own small garden in company with *R. campylogynum*, *R. pemakoense*, *R. ferrugineum*, *R.* 'Carmen' and a number of other dwarf rhododendrons – amongst which we also have *Cotoneaster congestus* 'Nana' and *Gaultheria procumbens* – and provides some necessary shade to the bed.

My wife Edith likes to have a flower or spray of something in season; the little vase on the kitchen windowsill is rarely empty, even in winter. *Viburnum bodnantense* 'Deben' outside the window provides a stem for the little vase inside, as does *Sarcococca humilis* by the back door, perfuming the room in

February. Self-sown seedlings come up at the base, fostered in the shade of the parent. At this time, too, another gem is in flower, *Helleborus purpurescens*, with its nodding dark purple blooms and conspicuous pale yellow stamens.

About ten years ago, we planted the rose 'Climbing Cécile Brunner' on the front wall of the house. It is now above the bedroom window and almost out of hand, but its glorious display of shell-pink buttonhole roses always makes us put off any drastic pruning, usually until a visit from the decorators is imminent, as downpipes and gutters are under the rose.

At the same time as the 'Cécile Brunner' is in flower, *Abutilon vitifolium* also unfolds its profusion of large single blooms of the softest shade of pale lavender. It is only a few yards from the rose, a lovely combination which was quite accidental – this was the warmest and most sheltered spot I could find for the handsome native of Chile. 'Alister Stella Gray' is a splendid buttonhole rose, for it flowers continuously from June to October; the small double flowers are borne in clusters, rich yellow, fading to white.

The back of our house has a small yard enclosed by walls. Here we have made a raised bed against the wall to provide the good drainage required by such charmers as *Saxifraga macnabiana*, *Sedum lydium*, *Saxifraga* 'Apiculata', *Daphne blagayana*, *D. tangutica*, *Corydalis chelianthifolia* and *Convolvulus mauritanicus* (*C. sabatius*). To brighten the walls, particularly in the winter months, we have variegated ivy 'Goldheart' and 'Paddy's Pride'.

In the planting of our own garden, I must confess there is always overcrowding; the desire for the newest aquisition is dominant over the need to give plants more room. This cannot be so in Sheffield Park. Here the eighteenth-century landscape has always to be taken into consideration; open space is very important, as are the vistas, focal points and peepholes. (We hope these do not look contrived, although they often are.) Where possible, planting is carried out on the perimeters of glades. Constant attention has to be given to plants, especially rhododendrons, which grow and encroach into views.

52

4.

5.

6.

4. The collection of Ghent azaleas at Sheffield Park is at its best in early June. 5. Thousands of spotted orchids now flower in a wild meadow set aside for native plants. Ajuga, betony, pulmonaria, ox-eyed daisies and a range of grasses also grow here. 6. Sheffield Park's autumn colour is justly famous and the Japanese maples at the first bridge are part of the original nineteenth-century planting. 7. July in the Stream Garden brings the red and white astilbes.

7.

Maxdene, Castle Cary, Somerset
Also Hadspen House, Castle Cary

ALAN EASON

It is quite usual for professional gardeners to create a garden for themselves which is in contrast to that of their employers. This has not happened in my case, partly because I had created and planted most of my own cottage garden in Castle Cary before going to Hadspen House in 1977.

My admiration for this great garden, which Mrs Penelope Hobhouse had restored from one originally created by her husband's grandmother in the early 1900s, depended very much on the fact that her ideas on planting and layout, with separate garden areas flowing into each other, coincided happily with my own, but on a much larger scale. Mrs Hobhouse is now at Tintinhull and is wonderfully extending her garden ideas there; for some time, however, she and I, as her gardener, worked closely and sympathetically in the Hadspen garden. It still engenders in me the feeling of romantic, overflowing ebullience, set as it is against a big bold massing of trees which frames the landscape.

My original apprenticeship was not in gardening at all but in my father's business as a butcher in Yeovil. The disciplines learned then are valuable now, especially as I am also running a nursery of 20,000 plants at Hadspen. Most of what I knew about horticulture as a child was picked up at the dinner table and on family garden trips. My father has a large greenhouse and was (still is) continually experimenting with a large range of plants, from oleanders to early lettuces. He will say that my interest took a long time to germinate but it was encouraged by opportunity.

When I was nineteen, Miss Monica Bell invited me to 'do something' about the garden of her seventeenth-century cottage, called Maxdene, in Castle Cary. She was seventy-eight and as her garden had become derelict and overgrown, she gave me a free hand to improve it. Through the garden, we became good friends and when Miss Bell died in 1973, she left me Maxdene and I developed this elongated half acre much as I had originally planned.

Someone described my garden recently as 'quirky' (not a word I would have used) but the feel of it probably goes along with the Bohemian character of the house.

The garden slopes uphill towards the east, separated from the house by a narrow courtyard but linked to it by a very old steep cobbled path. A stone retaining wall supports a rockery; the lawn, one of my two original features (the other being the winter garden) meets it at about eye level, seen from the house.

On the left of the path stands the conservatory, twenty-six feet high, which I built with the help of many friends over one year from the remains of a cottage which stood at a right angle to the house. A host of skills was needed, including welding, stone masonry, carpentry and bricklaying; because of the steep slope, it has been possible to have it virtually on two levels, with very tall plants like tree ferns (*Dicksonia antarctica*), bamboos, abutilons, *Lavatera bicolor* and, newly planted, *Cupressus cashmeriana*. The lower level is approached through a door on the ground floor of the house and the top door, also at ground level but at the top of the slope, leads into a balcony with an oriental white balus-

trade based on Chippendale's original designs for Chinese gates. This curves along the length of the building, bordered by a raised bed containing tender greenhouse shrubs like echiums, gloriously flowered with spikes of blue florets, oleanders and *Cassia corymbosa*, a golden-yellow-flowered shrub.

Beyond the conservatory is what is jokingly called my Zen Garden, an area which has changed many times following the demolition of yet another cottage. Having been pond, rockery and pleasaunce, it has now become a rectangular area of different-textured gravel shapes surrounded by paving around which are beds of colourful low plantings.

Over the years, the garden has defined itself into various areas, some almost completely enclosed, others flowing together and linking the garden. From nowhere can the whole be seen, so that there are always mysteries around the corner.

The winter garden, for example, is a paved area which is reached through an arch of euonymus from the Zen Garden. Although, amongst other things, it contains more than ten varieties of holly it is perhaps the most nearly formal area. Miss Bell thought I was mad to be so keen on holly (to her it was nasty, prickly stuff) but my botanical interest was awakening around that time. One of my discoveries is *Ilex* × *koehneana*, a marvellous foliage shrub with large glossy mid-green leaves, which is not grown often enough.

Here also are plants which are treasured for their winter flowers or their fragrance: snowdrops, bergenias, hellebores, cornus, wintersweet, *Lonicera*

. Alan Eason at Hadspen House.

fragrantissima, *L. standishii* and *Rho-dodendron* 'Christmas Cheer'. This last is a bit erratic about flowering; it gained its name by the fact that it can be forced by Christmas.

An area known as the vegetable garden wraps itself around two sides of the winter garden so that, here, herbs and vegetables grow alongside mahonias, fatsias and spring bulbs. The clothes-line is slung across the middle but even that is 'garden' because it has a wistaria taking over from one end and a Virginia creeper, wonderful in the autumn, from the other.

Beyond the winter garden runs the only straight path, through the long border and parallel with the garden wall. A line of columnar junipers is planted each side of it in the beds, breaking the line but also giving a vertical accent and reiterating the geometry of the wall and path. The beds are filled with all kinds of perennials and even fruit bushes like black currant; the path is edged with mellow old brick, as are all the paths, and, although these emphasize the straight lines, they are softened and broken by mounds of ground cover (sages, helichrysum, *Alchemilla mollis*) tumbling out on to the gravel path.

As many of my favourite plants were being used at Hadspen when I began

work there, I gained a tremendous number of ideas from the planting schemes. My employer, with her enthusiasm and imaginative use of colour and texture, introduced me to whole new genera of plants which I had previously overlooked: lovely herbaceous things like euphorbias to brighten the early spring days and rodgersias with their bold foliage.

The eight acres of Hadspen sit in a bowl sheltered from the north and east wind and, because of a line of old yew trees, the frost stays out of the main part of the garden. The garden had been virtually untouched for thirty years, and reclamation began in 1968; for seven years, Mrs Hobhouse did the work that had been done, earlier this century, by six gardeners; then Mr Eric Smith came along and I followed later. In order to save labour, the garden was turned into a place for shrubs and foliage, on several levels, like a theatre.

Flower colour was incidental; the aim was to provide an umbrella of shrubs with ground cover which fitted, pink or red, blue and grey.

Now that I run the garden at Hadspen, with the invaluable help of one other, the freedom is both exciting and frightening. One of the good things is that Mr Paul Hobhouse, my employer, allows me the freedom to plan and plant as I think fit. Although other areas are being developed completely afresh, much of the original planting is being carefully maintained; there is no point in changing for the sake of change.

I have planted a 'summer' border beside the long, south-facing brick wall in the kitchen garden where once were herbs and vegetables. In midsummer it is yellow and white with coreopsis, and showers of crambe, alchemilla and scabious. Later there are ceratostigmas and some of the more tender escallonias: *E. viscosa* (white) and *E. revoluta* (a very soft pink). A golden dell below the kitchen wall is now well under way using golden hostas, *Spiraea* 'Gold Flame', a golden catalpa, sambucus (the golden cut-leafed elder) and many other golden and yellow-foliaged plants.

The cottage garden behind the brick-walled water reservoir is now transformed from a muddly allotment into an area containing hollyhocks, delphiniums, foxgloves and lupins, but also plants like bergenias, eryngiums and hostas.

Hadspen is well known now for its hostas, as they have been grown here for some time. They are becoming popular partly because they are easy to grow on any soil; stately and architectural, their foliage is much prized by devotees of floral art, especially because they come in a large range of colours, sizes, shapes and variegation. Since becoming a keen member of the Hosta Society, I have been putting them in for competition; one of our first successes was at the Liverpool Garden Festival where we picked up prizes with 'Phyllis Campbell', medium sized with striking cream colorations on mid-green leaves, and 'Frances Williams', which is big with gold-margined blue corrugated leaves.

2.

3.

4.

5.

6.

The gardens change all the time and a lot of the enjoyment is in the fact that I am allowed to go on changing them. It is very stimulating; who knows what the future will bring?

2. Hadspen's Victorian fountain pond, overlooked by a young specimen of *Cornus controversa* 'Variegata', is fully planted around with herbaceous perennials like rodgersias, hostas, astilbes, rheums and irises.   3. Evening sunlight on the wall of Hadspen's peach walk highlights the single plant of *Clematis montana* spreading far along it.   4. Perennial sweet peas and *Alstroemeria ligtu* at Hadspen House form the foreground to this view over the lily pond and bold foliage plants to the Somerset countryside. *Gunnera manicata, Salix fargesii* and *Peltiphyllum peltatum* thrive with grasses including the plumes of *Stipa gigantea*.   5. At Maxdene the Zen Garden in May is bright with plants like foxgloves and aquilegia with *Laburnum* 'Vossii' behind.   6. Next to the pale pink of *Jasminum polyanthum*, the clusters of the mauve flowers of *Abutilon vitifolium* 'Suntense' show up well in Alan Eason's conservatory.   7. Soft fruit on the left of the path and herbaceous plantings of *Dierama pulcherrimum, Senecio monroi*, dorycnium and the red *Leycesteria formosa* on the right flourish against the south garden wall at Maxdene.

7.

Westminster Abbey Gardens, London

MARIAN COUCHMAN, BEM

The gardens of Westminster Abbey have complemented the Abbey buildings from the days when the first church was built by Edward the Confessor and consecrated on 25 December 1065, for at that time College Garden was growing herbs for both medicinal and culinary purposes for the monks' daily life – this area of land, about an acre, has been under continuous cultivation for over nine hundred years.

The gardens are not large by many gardens' standards – they cover little

1. Marian Couchman.

over three acres in all, being subdivided into six areas. The Great Cloister, the churchyard of St Margaret's Church and Dean's Yard, once the farmyard of the monastery, are now lawn areas. With the millions of tourists that arrive annually from all over the world the lawns receive very hard wear, especially in the summer when we have a warm spell of sunshine and weary legs and bodies require a place to rest. The grass in Dean's Yard is a play area for the boys of the Abbey Choir School and Westminster School. From the early 1970s to the 1980s the exterior of the great church has been cleaned and restored. During this time, as work progressed, sections of lawn have been taken from the gardens to give storage space for stone, scaffolding and security fencing and then, after a two-to-three-year period, returned to the gardeners to reinstate as lawn. None of the lawns are of fine fescue or agrostis grasses – most areas contain a high percentage of *Poa annua*. Although this 'dies out' during a hot summer it soon regenerates when the autumn rains fall. All the lawns have the same annual treatment, an application of slow-acting spring fertilizer with an analysis of 3N:6P:6K to increase the root formation of grass and therefore enabling the grass to survive longer during dry weather. The broad-leaved weeds are kept suppressed by selective liquid weedkiller and on the large lawn areas a combined fertilizer/weedkiller in granular form is used.

The trees around the Abbey were all planted during the last century. Over 80 per cent are *Platanus × hispanica*, London plane, as they were found to be the most suitable trees to thrive in the polluted London air in Victorian and Edwardian days. Many of the oldest trees in College Garden, Dean's Yard and St Margaret's Churchyard are very fine specimens and have been allowed to grow naturally, giving the true shape of the species – upright main branches and pendulous laterals gracefully falling towards the ground. Since being at Westminster I have had to plant a London plane in St Margaret's Churchyard after two semi-mature trees were killed by gas leaking from the mains. In Dean's Yard I have aimed to give the area a greater variety of tree form and leaf shape. Today the yard contains a *Sorbus aria* (whitebeam) planted to commemorate the first flower festival staged by NAFAS in 1966. The *Catalpa bignonioides* (Indian bean) was planted by the Worshipful Company of Gardeners in 1973. To add to the foliage variation an *Acer drummondii* was given by Dr Douglas Guest on his retirement from the Abbey where he was organist and master of the choristers. College Garden is blessed with trees which are well situated in that open space. In the late 1970s a *Metasequoia glyptostroboides* was planted in College Garden by the Friends of Richard St Barbe-Baker ('the Man of the Trees'). It seemed appropriate to plant that ancient tree in the old garden. It was only known in fossil form until a living tree was found in the early 1940s in China; it has since spread rapidly throughout the world. The row of mature Japanese cherry trees is the main feature of College Garden when they are in flower about the third week in April.

The air in London is now called 'clean' though it is more correct to say hat it is sulphur free. A disadvantage is that we no longer have a continuous sulphur fungicide falling on our plants, so black spot affects our roses, rust is on the hollyhocks and the London plane trees have anthracnose fungus, which attacks the young leaves as they open in the spring; the affected leaves then fall, giving a light leaf fall throughout the summer.

The Little Cloister garden must be one of the most photographed areas of London, with its old gas lamps, attractive wrought-iron gate and railings and the central fountain with its water falling into a rectangular fish pond. The cloister dates back about three hundred years; judging by old drawings and photographs the layout of the garden has changed little over the last century. The fountain was installed about 1840 and a photograph dated about 1880 shows the perimeter border as we have it today. Only small L-shaped corners were grassed then – the rest of the area was paved. Few flowers were grown in the garden before 1930 as a London plane tree dominated the area, taking light from the houses and garden. The only plants were ferns and evergreens. Today the aim is to have as many flowers as possible in the garden, for as long as possible. Being only a small rectangle adjacent to buildings, one half is in full sun, when it shines, and the other never sees the sun. In this area plants tend to run to leaf and are slow to flower if we have a wet spring. The sunny side dries out very quickly and on some days it requires watering twice. The soil throughout the area is very poor; it is really only a sooty deposit in which to place the plants. Over the years as much compost as possible has been incorporated into the ground in the autumn with a dressing of bonemeal. Before the summer bedding is planted a balanced fertilizer, with an analysis of $7N:5P:7K$, is forked into the ground. When working to a budget items such as fertilizer and equipment must be considered carefully. After much experimenting, the plants used today in the summer bedding schemes are the

geranium cultivar 'Wembley Gem' and the fuchsia cultivar 'Mrs Rundle'; both bush and standard plants are used to get a variation in height. The edging plants are French marigolds, alyssum, *Begonia semperflorens* and impatiens. A few 'dot' plants of *Cineraria maritima* and *Nicotiana affinis* 'Lime Green' give added interest. The summer bedding plants are grown in a small glasshouse in College Garden. The space is very limited for these requirements, but with temporary cold frames during the spring period enough protected space is available.

Late spring frosts are rare in central London but the main problem is the poor light during the winter and early spring, which is not conducive to good plant growth. The spring display in the Little Cloister is provided by daffodils, usually a large trumpet variety such as 'Unsurpassable' or 'Rembrandt'; these are weather-resistant cultivars with stiff stems that resist the wind that eddies round the buildings. The daffodils are interplanted with April-flowering tulips, thus giving colour from mid-March to the end of April.

To the east of the Little Cloister is our new garden. This was created in the late 1950s in the ruins of the Norman chapel of St Catherine, the infirmary chapel of the monastery. The chapel fell into ruin about 1540 and after some years a canons' house was built on the site. This house was burnt down during the Second World War. When rebuilt, the houses were smaller and the old chapel ruin was left as an extra garden. The Norman column bases are set in grass at approximately the chapel's floor level. Today the central and north aisle are garden and one day the south aisle will be uncovered for all to see. The main feature in the spring is the *Magnolia stellata* with its white star-like flowers. Through the summer months a bed of 'Queen Elizabeth' roses gives an ever-reliable display of colour.

The most ancient of the open spaces around the Abbey is College Garden, the old herb garden of the monastery. This acre of land has never been built on

and today it is bounded on the south and east sides by the old wall that kept the River Thames out of the monastery that was built on Thorney Island. This garden was private to the Dean and Chapter of Westminster until its nine-hundredth anniversary in 1966, when the garden was opened to the public one day a week; every Thursday since then many people have found pleasure and relaxation in the garden. The lawns in the area have the same annual maintenance as the other grass areas around the Abbey. The lawns are free of flowerbeds as the area is used for garden parties. As the garden was the old herb garden, herbs have been planted in the various borders. In 1980 the British Herb Association offered a collection of old English herbs. After giving the offer some thought a small bed near the north gate of the garden was cleared of other plant material and a herb bed was created. We have no records of the plants that were originally grown but we feel that some of the herbs planted there now must have been grown in the garden in its early days – they include thyme, hyssop, rosemary, bay, rue, marjoram and germander. The main borders are mixed shrub and herbaceous underplanted with spring bulbs. These areas are more colourful in the spring before the ground becomes overshadowed by the mature plane trees.

During the construction of a new border at the south end of the garden during the cold winter of 1962 two archways were noticed in the old monastery perimeter wall. On looking at early plans of the area it could be seen that the monks had their fish ponds at the south end of the garden and outside the wall ran the mill stream which must have fed the ponds with water.

In June the small rose garden adds colour to the area. The central beds contain the cultivar 'Mary Sumner' (the founder of the Mothers' Union). This variety was introduced in 1976 to celebrate the hundredth anniversary of the founding of the Union. The cultivar is a small-flowered floribunda of an intense orange-red in colour. The young half-opened buds are ideal for table decoration.

People may say that no major alterations have been made in the garden layout during my twenty years plus at Westminster, but when working within an area with nine hundred years of history, twenty years are but a fragment in time. The open ground around the Abbey is an intrinsic part of the establishment today, with its sports area and pleasure gardens, just as it was in monastic times when it was farmyard and herb garden.

Gardening in London is a law unto itself and, coming as I did from the Nottingham University School of Agriculture and maintaining grounds at a teachers' training college in Buckinghamshire, and after many years of growing chrysanthemums for both cut flowers and for the plant trade, working in the centre of a city with its polluted atmosphere and poor light conditions in the winter months made me rethink some of my horticultural principles. If I have missed anything while at the Abbey it has been visiting, in the country, the major flower shows which stage displays of early and late-flowering chrysanthemums.

2.

3.

2. Spring in the College Garden.　3. Monks grew herbs here nine hundred years ago and this bed includes bay, rosemary, rue, hyssop, marjoram, thymes and lavender.　4. Summer in the Little Cloister.　5. College Garden is at its best in the spring: this year the bullfinches had made several good meals of the blossom buds of the white cherry. The tulips are 'Apeldoorn'.

4.

5.

Great Comp Cottage, Borough Green, Sevenoaks, Kent

STEPHEN H. G. ANDERTON

Great Comp is a seven-acre garden of decidedly all-year interest. Its attraction for me is that it is packed with good plants and has real personality. It is no park – it is the result of the work of two people, Mr and Mrs Roderick Cameron, who began it from scratch in 1957. It is still a two-man garden so far as the maintenance is concerned, although it requires more effort than that to keep the garden open to the public every day from April to October.

Great Comp has no employees. I have been maintaining the garden with Mr Cameron on a free-lance contractual basis since 1982. But my work here can include anything from cutting grass to lecturing and giving garden tours in French! Everyone does a bit of everything and paperwork is strictly confined to the necessary minimum. Since November 1982 the garden itself has been made a charitable trust, thereby ensuring its future.

It is a young garden, now in the flush of its first maturity. But here and there places are just beginning to require reappraisal and rejuvenation.

One such area is a dell in the centre of the garden, where a *Rhododendron thomsonii* recently died, leaving a good space for new herbaceous planting. Here I am trying to create the effect of a bog garden – but without the water, for the site is by no means wet, although it becomes temporarily soggy in bad weather. I have planted a 'river' of herbaceous plants running from the shade at the back, along the foot of a small rock bluff, to a seat by the path. With a bit of luck, when *Magnolia sinensis* gets going, you will be able to sit here and look up into its pendant flowers or down

into the 'river'. Below the seat in the shallows is the creeping woodland *Phlox stolonifera* in various forms, underplanted with sanguinaria and dodecatheon. Behind are the stronger shapes of rodgersia, osmunda, candelabra primulas, and a host of different irises. These will flower for about eight weeks; notably they include *Iris fulva*, whose frequent reluctance to do very much at all seems to be forgotten here and it produces its unusual orange-terracotta flowers with enthusiasm. There are also several forms of the Japanese *Iris ensata*, including some wild bicolours. Room had to be found somewhere for *Iris* 'Gerald Darby', which might almost be described as a hedging iris, so strong is its growth and its four-foot-tall black stems, topped with an endless succession of blue flowers. 'Gerald Darby' is one of those paragons which, welcome or not, grow in spite of what you do to them.

The whole is backed by established azaleas, tree heaths and an amelanchier, all helping to make quite a splash in the spring.

My own private garden at Great Comp is in what used to be the stable yard, between my house, which is a Victorian extension of the main house, and the stable, now a small concert hall. When I worked in Cambridgeshire on cold clay, I used to long to get my hands on some sheltered little oasis, full of architectural interest, with a cooperative soil – and warmth. My luck was in – here I have just that.

But even the yard was not immune to the ravages of the 1981–2 winter. When I took over, the beds, though well established, had several wounds to

nurse. Fortunately, the casualties did not include a splendid tree-like specimen of *Berberis valdiviana* which fills one sheltered corner of the yard by the well.

In the centre of the cobbles is an island bed which I am endeavouring to make into a kind of rich *maquis*. Definitely not scree – there is enough hardness in the yard already and I do not want to see bare earth between the plants either. Instead I am filling it with low mounds of all kinds – mats, mounds, sprawlers, lollers – rubbing, I hope, carefully contrasting shoulders. Here I can garden on a small scale, finding space for rarities, even obscurities, and simple favourites.

One of my great passions is species irises and, not surprisingly, the season in the yard begins with them. The Juno group thrives in this hot sandy soil and *Iris bucharica, magnifica* and × *warsind* flower prolifically – if anything better than the easier winter-flowering *Iris unguicularis*, which is just as keen a sunbather.

I have several Evansia irises here too, notably that splendidly blue Burmese form of *Iris tectorum* and, nestling under a large wintersweet, *Iris confusa*, which has cane-like stems and might at first be taken for a bamboo or a palm. But the queen of the Evansias must be *Iris* 'Bourne Graceful', a cross between two forms of *Iris japonica*. Its tall sprays of orchid-like blooms are a crisp mixture of blue, white and ochre, like a Minoan fresco. To see it is to want it. (A fine thing for our nursery trade!)

Thrift is here, of course, and helianthemums, but you have to get down on your knees to appreciate *Scilla autumnalis* and *Iris attica*. To break up a

. Stephen Anderton, Great Comp, beside *Sequoia sempervirens* 'Cantab'.

straight paved edge I use a tender succulent, *Aptenia cordifolia*, which I put out in May as a rooted cutting and by November it has covered two square yards with a one-inch mat of bright green studded with small red daisies. Sadly, one good frost and it looks like washed-up seaweed.

Against the house wall I have clusters of large terracotta pots which are put out in summer. Some hold plants to give height, an orange or an oleander, others contain a mixture of colourful fragrant flowers intertwined with a foil of luxuriant foliage. When you put a plant in a pot you say, 'Look, here is something special!', so it has to look good and rich. *Helichrysum petiolatum* has become ubiquitous as a grey foil in such schemes, following the fine example of Sissinghurst. I like to roll

some of their ideas together and grow *Diplacus glutinosus*, *Begonia sutherlandii* and the yellow *Helichrysum petiolatum* all together in one pot. The orange flowers blend perfectly and reach a peak in September.

The rather more reserved grey *Helichrysum microphyllum* I grow with pink trailing carnations from the Tyrol. Their perfume of cloves is so strong it will fill the air on warm evenings.

On a grander scale *Pelargonium tomentosum*, the peppermint geranium, makes another good foil with its broad hairy leaves. I like it with *Begonia pendula* or purple petunias, which always smell stronger than the other colours.

For a place where a subtler scheme will suffice, the ordinary grey *Helichrysum petiolatum* looks very distinguished with *Sphaeralcea munroana*,

another sub-shrub which sprawls about in the same manner, but has cut silvery leaves and endless one-inch mallow-like flowers of a lovely old-red-brick colour. Unfortunately it is completely camouflaged against my brick walls.

Incidentally Great Comp's only bit of ground elder grows in the yard. It is variegated, and grows in a wide jardinière on the shady side. It appears not to revert and to be a slow spreader. On these accounts it is tempting to try it in the ground but I can imagine that without the confines of a pot it would turn green overnight and romp away in all directions.

I try to make sure there are plenty of night-scented plants in the yard because when the music festival is on it becomes in effect an extension of the foyer, where people can wander with drinks

during the intervals. *Mirabilis jalapa* is usually full of its bright trumpets by the time the September concerts come round. Cooperative to the last, the blooms wait until late afternoon before they even open.

The concerts are an important part of life at Great Comp, as we are all music lovers as well as gardeners. Before turning to gardening I graduated in drama and classics and when time allows, which alas is all too seldom, I enjoy writing piano and chamber music, so I suppose I am an hybrid well matched to the set-up here.

Not least because of my own background, I am convinced that serious gardening can be an art form like any other, and that an appreciation of other forms is invaluable in sharpening one's sensibilities for the use of form, colour, texture, scale and so on. And by gardening – what I call 'real' gardening – I mean the *making* and the *refining* of excellent gardens, from the planning right through to the planting and weeding, regardless of size or scale. It is a different and more complete process than either pure maintenance or landscape management and design. Perhaps this is because a gardener can be in touch with the whole creative process. He is his own architect, clerk of works, builder, navvy and, finally, occupant. So he ought to be aware of all the hidden problems and possible solutions. And if on top of this he has a clear idea of the effect he wants to create, should he not then be able to do wonders?

2. In the dell Stephen has created a river of plants and the creamy-white plumes of *Rodgersia pinnata* flower behind the terracotta *Iris fulva*, the bluish-purple *Iris* 'Gerald Darby' and *Primula florindae*.   3. The dell on an autumn evening, backed by an amelanchier and *Cotinus americanus*.   4. *Iris* 'Bourne Graceful' is one of the Evansias, crested irises which are the beginning of a new generation of hybrids.
5. *Magnolia liliiflora* 'Nigra' in front of Great Comp.   6. Stephen Anderton's yard by Great Comp Cottage contains a succession of favourite plants throughout the spring and summer. Here are *Osteospermum jucundum*, *Iris* 'Rudskyi' and flax. The potentilla is 'Moonlight'.

2.

5.

Fern Cottage, Holme, nr Carnforth, Lancashire

CLIVE JONES

1. Clive Jones at his Friday job at Fairthwaite Park below Casterton Fell.

When my father was recalled to the colours in 1939 he entrusted his Herefordshire grocery business to my mother and his garden to me. For the next six years I made a modest contribution to the nation's 'Dig for Victory' campaign and in so doing gained a love of working with the soil and with the seasons that has never left me.

After twenty-two years as an army officer in Somerset, Malaya, Hampshire, Hong Kong, Westphalia and Lancashire, I decided to resign from the army, go to horticultural college for a year and then earn my living in amenity horticulture. I shall always be grateful to Norman Entwistle, head gardener at Cuerden Hall, near Preston, for the generosity with which he taught me his skills and the tricks of the trade; also for the support and encouragement he gave me while I was making the transition from army officer to gardener.

We moved to a cottage in the south Lakeland, built in 1820 alongside the Kendal–Preston canal to house one of the canal-keepers. The garden was well on its way back to the jungle. It is in a bit of a frost-pocket and the rhododendrons, pieris and pachysandra struggling for existence screamed high alkalinity. On the credit side it was fairly roomy, or so I thought then. The whole site, including the house, is about three-quarters of an acre; there is a very good depth of light loamy soil which is well drained and a pleasure to work. Surrounding two sides of the triangle were well-made hedges of thorn, ash and bullace, while the northern side boasted a five-foot high drystone wall sixty yards long. Around the whole periphery was a fair sprinkling of thirty-year-old Lawson and Sawara cypress cultivars, including the golden Lawson, *Chamaecyparis lawsoniana* 'Lanei', and feathery *C.l.* 'Fletcheri'. Dominating the southern end was a forty-foot Scots pine (under which my wife's woodland garden of violets, aconites, ferns and lily of the valley now thrives).

Soon after moving to Fern Cottage I spent a year at horticultural college; I came away from it full of enthusiasm, ready to tackle my own garden and eager to establish myself in the south Lakeland gardening world.

I had been fascinated by bonsai ever since I had first encountered these little trees at the Southport Show a few years earlier. Several of the southern bonsai nurseries had exhibits there and I had found their displays quite enchanting. I now started to sell bonsai trees myself; at that time there was nowhere in the north of England where you could buy a bonsai tree, so I had virtually no competition. Furthermore, bonsai gave me wet-weather work, and in an area with an average rainfall of fifty inches this was very important.

I had by then decided that I wanted to work the year round in four or five good-quality gardens on a one-day-a-week basis, as I wanted a variety of locations and people. Within six months I had my four gardens, all of them in beautiful locations. The first is a two-acre garden surrounding an elegant old house at the foot of the Casterton Fell on the North Yorkshire/Lancashire border. The main features of the garden are a half-acre lawn, with herbaceous border surrounds, extensive wall plantings and three rose gardens.

The second of my gardens is at the Levens Hall dower house, situated at the mouth of the River Kent on the north-eastern corner of Morecambe Bay. The one-and-a-half-acre garden is surrounded on two sides by Levens Park. Oak, beech and sycamore trees abound, making winter leaf clearance a never-ending task. The main features are the mixed borders full of the very best ornamental species and cultivars of small trees, shrubs and herbaceous plants. In mid-spring the garden is superb, ablaze with the colour of a large variety of narcissi, fritillarias and flowering cherries. Working here on a warm early May day is my idea of heaven.

The third job to be offered to me was at the village of Barrows Green, just across the hill from Levens, an old farmhouse in lovely rolling Westmorland countryside. The owner is a well known flower arranger and show judge and I have learnt a lot from him.

My fourth job takes me twenty miles away to North Yorkshire, to the village of Lower Bentham, which has the river Wenning running through it. Here is the one-acre walled garden of a very popular little restaurant, beautifully landscaped with Silverdale limestone. Within reason, expense was no object and once I had proved myself I had a completely free hand. I found the challenge of providing flowers for the restaurant for at least seven months of the year very satisfying.

These gardens are still my main source of income. I have been tempted with other offers but have been unable to tear myself away from these four. I have repeatedly worked every square inch of all of them, I know their plants well and, perhaps more important, their owners equally well.

Much as I have come to love these gardens, however, my first love is my own garden. It gives me endless pleasure and, since we have opened to the public on four days a year under the Gardeners' Benevolent Society's charity scheme, I have been able to share this pleasure with others.

Good gardening, like good soldiering, is primarily a question of basics – in the case of gardening, soil preparation, structure and pH, windbreaks and weed control. I could not do much about the soil pH except steer clear of the calcifuges. My camellias and pieris were going to have to be tub plantings around the house. Double digging with liberal applications of well-rotted farm manure did much for the soil structure. Getting rid of perennial weeds took over a year and there was no way I was going to start planting until this had been achieved. Fortunately, glyphosate (Roundup) had just come on to the market and this, as I have proved many times over, is the complete answer to all perennial weeds except nettles.

The garden was to consist of a continuous flow of island beds, in which plantings were to be at three levels – tree, shrub, ground. Particular attention was to be given to shape, form and colour combinations. Evergreen and deciduous plants were going to be in proportion of one to three. Only the best cultivars were to be planted when it was at all possible to obtain them and this was going to mean a lot of research and shopping around. But above all it was going to be an all-the-year-round garden. At all times I want colour and flower.

It is easy to achieve a colourful garden in June and July but midwinter is a bit more challenging. January and February are the 'down' months and any plant that can give the morale a boost over the post-Christmas period is to be treasured. For me there are four groupings of winter-interest plants. First there are the flowers: such treasures as *Helleborus foetidus*, *H. orientalis* and *H. niger*, *Viburnum fragrans* and *V. bodnantense*, *Mahonia bealei* and *M.* 'Charity', hamamelis, particularly *H. mollis* and its cultivars, *Jasminum nudiflorum*, the winter-flowering cultivars of *Erica carnea* and, of course, the early flowering bulbs.

Then there are the berries and catkins: pyracantha and cotoneaster on the walls, heavy with red and orange fruits;

white and pink-berried pernettias; *Garrya elliptica* 'James Roof', quite stunning with its mass of four-inch long tassles; and the corkscrew hazel, *Corylus avellana* 'Contorta', with its dangling lambs' tails.

Next there are the barks which show up so well in winter; *Prunus serrula* with its polished red-brown mahogany-like bark; the paperbark maple, *Acer griseum*, and the coral bark, *A. palmatum* 'Senkaki'; the snakebarks, some of which I have, including *A. pennsylvanicum*, which is beautifully striped with white and jade green, *A. hersii*, with its wonderfully marbled bark, and *A. rufinerve*, with its conspicuous white striations. The crimson-stalked *Cornus alba* 'Sibirica', the Westonbirt dogwood, is most striking, but prettiest of all is the Himalayan birch, *Betula jaquemontii*, dazzling you with its white stems.

Finally, the mainstay of my winter garden is the conifer. Apart from my conifer specimen plantings, I have three conifer rockeries whose winter colourings never fail to thrill me. The golden Scots pine, the Siberian microbiota, the Japanese red cedar, *Cryptomeria japonica* 'Elegans' and the 'Pembury Blue' Lawson cypress all colour well; also the Arizona cork-bark fir, *Abies lasiocarpa*, the little cypress, *Chamaecyparis pisifera* 'Snow', and the best of all golden conifers, *C. obtusa* 'Nana Aurea'.

Without question my favourite genus is the acer. I am devoted to my maples and am gradually acquiring a good collection of them. Of all the tree families Aceraceae must surely provide the most splendid array of the exciting and the colourful. To me they are the aristocrats of the tree world; no other tree family can offer the same diversity of height and shape, colour of leaf and beauty of bark. (Rhododendron enthusiasts would not agree.) Over two hundred cultivars are now in existence and many of them can be obtained from John Jackson at Bamber Bridge, Preston. Their leaf colours range from pale pink and white to purple; in garden

2.

3.

rockery and bonsai plantings I have about sixty cultivars, some of them very rare.

I love camellias and pieris so much that I make an annual spring pilgrimage to Wakehurst Place and Sheffield Park just to see the very fine collections of these, which seem to thrive so well in West Sussex. Visits to famous gardens have influenced me much in my choice of plants. I remember after a spring visit to Sissinghurst eagerly wanting to get back home to seek out and plant a *Sorbus cashmiriana*. I already had *S.* 'Joseph Rock' and *S. vilmorinii*, but having seen *S. cashmiriana* flowering at Sissinghurst I felt I could not live without it. It is surprising just what you can get into three-quarters of an acre and have yet to fail to find room for a plant. My latest passion is for the old China roses. I got 'Cécile Brunner', 'Jenny Wren' and 'Sophie's Perpetual' from Scott Merriot early on. I'm about to add to them with 'Old Blush China', 'Mutabilis' and 'Perle d'Or' from David Austin. Some new, exciting, shade-tolerant plants from Beth Chatto will liven up the woodland garden; one of them is the variegated strawberry which I thought so enchanting as a ground-cover planting on a trip we made to Knightshayes last autumn.

I have had some upsets and minor disasters but it is surprising how resilient gardeners are; they have to be or they would give up. Fortunately all the big mistakes I have made have been in my own garden. I now treat creosote with great respect, having killed three valued maples by putting them too close to some recently treated stakes in hot weather. I check, double-check and check again before I use a knapsack sprayer – four years ago I killed off a fair-sized patch of one of my lawns before I realized I was using Gramoxone, not Verdone. I gave daily thanks for weeks after that I had done it to my own lawn and not to one of my clients'. I think worst of all was the winter of 1981–2. I lost a lot of treasured plants that winter and even now do not care to think too much about the

68

horror of it all. When the temperature plunged to −18°C I knew I was going to lose hebes, choisyas, garryas and camellias, but some leycesterias, pyracanthas, cupressus and acers also succumbed. Hopefully we will not have a repeat of it for many years to come.

I am so grateful to gardening. I often marvel that I am being paid for doing something that I would be doing anyway. My work keeps me physically and spiritually healthy. Through it I have made very many friends and gained lots of interest. It is a complete way of life throughout the year. In winter I have my horticultural society and Women's Institute lecturing; in spring my garden visits down south; in summer my horticultural shows and bonsai exhibiting; and in autumn a holiday from it all and a chance to recoup and come back fresh for another gardening year. As long as I keep my health I will never have to retire and this is a very considerable bonus in today's world. My army years are now very remote, almost as if they happened in another life. If I have one regret it is that I did not make the change earlier, but then, as they say, better late than never.

2. May, 7 a.m. In this plantsman's garden *Acer palmatum* 'Beni Komachi' (the red, beautiful little girl) is at bottom right and, by the bend in the path, is Clive Jones's favourite golden foliage shrub *Sambucus racemosa* 'Plumosa Aurea'.　3. Spencer variety sweet peas lead into the canal shrubbery, at the end of which are the seed heads of *Rheum palmatum* 'Atrosanguineum', glorious in early spring.　4. His love of plants is evident in this view towards the Hutton Roof limestone escarpment. The larch archway is covered with rose 'American Pillar'.　5. The Rose Walk (including 'Albéric Barbier', 'Dr W. van Fleet' and 'Queen Elizabeth') is underplanted with not-so-hardy perennials like *Calceolaria rugosa*, *Fuchsia* 'Tom Thumb', *Chrysanthemum frutescens* and *Dahlia* 'Red Pygmy'.　6. All Clive's bonsai are more than forty years old, three being *Acer palmatum* cultivars. At the centre is the much-prized 'Deshojo', brilliant red in spring, with, right, 'Kiyohime' and, left, 'Shigitatsu Sawa', a cultivar which dates back to 1700.

5.

6.

Churchtown Farm Field Studies Centre, Lanlivery, Bodmin, Cornwall

PETER MACFADYEN

The design of the gardens at Churchtown Farm presented a unique challenge. What was required was a teaching garden that was aesthetically pleasing; a garden filled with surprises and excitement, and most important of all, one accessible to disabled people. The horticultural side also had to dovetail in with a wide range of other environmental and outdoor activities. Now, seven years after its conception, I believe most of the objectives have been largely achieved, although the requirement for an instant garden was more difficult – it will remain a new garden well into the 1990s.

The decision of the Spastics Society to establish a Field Studies Centre for all types of disabled people was a very brave one. The Centre could be regarded as a luxury, but was felt to be one that the Society should afford. When fifteen acres of land and old farm buildings were donated in 1973, they set about an expensive and lavish conversion that resulted in a Field Studies Centre well equipped by any standards. With later expansion, provision was made for up to sixty disabled people and their staff, groups coming for one-week courses throughout the year. With a laboratory, library, art, craft, photography and meeting rooms as well as a heated swimming pool and all the kitchen and laundry facilities required, the tiny village of Lanlivery found itself host to a thriving new community.

The Centre's land runs down to a stream, and a nature reserve with full wheelchair access was developed alongside it. A small farm with a wide range of animals has always been an important part of the work, and this took up most of the remaining land. With these facilities, and the whole of Cornwall as an additional classroom, the Centre was soon providing activities including bird watching, pond and seashore ecology, and local natural history and archaeology. To complement this, outdoor activities – sailing, canoeing, rock climbing and walking – were all introduced. No one is considered too severely disabled to attend courses, and no one too young or too old. Roughly equal numbers of mentally and physically handicapped people visit the Centre, and in 1984 they numbered nearly two thousand.

Dr Mike Cotton, the Centre's first warden, was behind the rapid expansion. It often happens that a client is willing to spend huge sums of money on buildings and an insignificant amount on landscaping and plants. Dr Cotton, a keen gardener himself, was, however, well aware of the need to rectify the negligible planting and landscape work around the impressive buildings. It was in this context that I first came to Churchtown, in a voluntary capacity, to help 'sort out' the gardens. At the time I was part way through my horticulture degree course at Reading University, having previously been employed at Ness Gardens near Liverpool.

I fell in love with Cornwall, and also became aware of the potential for the use of plants in the improvement of disabled people's lives. The Centre acquired the old vicarage, and with this came roughly a third of an acre of gently sloping land – a mass of nettles, docks and granite. I planned the landscaping for this area as a major part of my degree course. At much the same time, Churchtown hosted a seminar for people working within the field of horticulture and plants; a whole new concept, that of 'horticultural therapy', was beginning to emerge in Britain as I started work on the gardens at Churchtown.

Right from the start I was aiming to produce an interesting and beautiful garden, not a 'disabled garden'. To me that conjures up a picture of virus infected plants, trees that have been wrongly pruned and specimens such as *Salix tortuosa*! I was also against a garden of raised beds at just the right height for wheelchair users (but difficult to grow in), stating for all to see 'This garden is for disabled people.' The gardens that have evolved do have raised beds and sunken paths, but these are a part of the overall design in which the disability angle becomes coincidental – the gardens are for everyone to work in and enjoy.

I inherited a number of flowerbeds and planted areas, most of which had been either neglected or misused. In the central courtyard of the main building is one of the finest examples I know of 'an architect's raised bed' – stark concrete sides at a height that means someone in a wheelchair has their chin resting on the top, sited in a wind tunnel and filled with builders' rubble and subsoil. One side is a useful rockery and now, four years after I planted prostrate and dwarf conifers there, it is at last becoming a presentable feature.

Much of my time initially was spent on tasks such as the removal of sycamore and larch planted adjacent to buildings. I joined together two small

Lettuces, originally raised in peat blocks from pelleted seeds, being planted by Peter Macfadyen and a group of physically handicapped children in a raised bed built from granite found in the garden.

lasshouses, sited in full sun and with oor wheelchair access, to form a tunnel f glass. One end now contains a fine ollection of cacti – my desert – and the ther, 'tropical' plants including ba-anas, bromeliads, *Mimosa pudica* (the ensitive plant) and passion fruit. To eople who spend most of their lives in omes or hospital beds, forcing their vay through this lush undergrowth resents a whole new world of stimu-ation and excitement.

The biggest challenge in building Churchtown's teaching gardens has een the range of clients with whom I vork. In one week I normally have five roups of disabled people for just one ay each; this gives six hours in which o introduce the whole concept of lants, perhaps teach some simple tech-iques and hopefully produce a long-erm motivation from a short, sharp timulation. Those five groups may ange from highly intelligent people vho are severely physically disabled to eople who are very acutely mentally lisabled. My work is to find what these eople *can* do, and to show them how.

My first priority was to ensure that his could continue in all weathers, and we built a large wooden glasshouse to act as my classroom. Within this the tables are on wheels and the floor paved to give maximum adaptability. I estab-lished a large fuchsia collection and a wide range of other plants which are easy to grow and easy to propagate. Fuchsias are turgid enough to enable someone with poor hand control to take cuttings and are particularly easy to maintain. I grow a range of food crops, and some, such as loofahs, for interest. In general I have stayed clear of special equipment and complex adaptations, the object being to encourage people to do it themselves at home without great expense. Peat blocks and pelleted seeds have proved particularly useful (both developed for commercial horticul-ture). I have watched with great pleasure as people whose only coordi-nation is in their feet sow pelleted let-tuce or plant out lettuce in blocks into the garden. These are real and impor-tant achievements for individuals whose lives are dominated by what they cannot do.

The other building in the garden is a purpose-built potting-shed. This has a bench fitted to an old wheelchair lift that can be adjusted to suit anyone, an extensive library, and facilities to show slides and to study plants in great depth. The potting-shed is built into the per-gola which runs from the greenhouse. I particularly wanted a tunnel of plants – a half-way stage between an indoor room and the outside world. Clematis, lonicera, vines, dutchman's pipe, wis-taria and a number of roses climb up and over. The roses are part of an extensive collection of old-fashioned plants. They represent the best of each group within the roses and are a good example of planting that can suit a number of levels: I can spend hours discussing the genetics and breeding of roses with some people who share the fascination, or use the colours and scents to stimu-late a less able visitor – the scent of the leaves of *R. eglanteria*, strongly rem-iniscent of apples, for example, is always a surprise, and a hundred 'Europeana' floribundas in front of the old vicarage are a blaze of colour from June to October.

The roses take up a long bed on one side of the pergola; on the other, twenty or so vegetables are displayed. In gen-eral I grow vegetables throughout the

71

2. Overlooked by Lanlivery Parish Church, the herb garden in the main teaching area contains German camomile and bronze fennel as well as bergamot, oregano, savories, angelica, lovage and Jerusalem artichoke beyond.

3. The St Austell Rotary Club built and financed the water garden to Peter Macfadyen's design and planting plans. Cordylines, bay and tree sage flourish in a corner almost completely free from frost.

garden – runner beans climb trees, yellow courgettes act as ground cover, rhubarb, chard, sweetcorn and tomatoes are all used as ornamentals. So often these attractive plants are relegated to a hidden corner – the tomato (originally called 'love apple') was grown for many years as an ornamental before anyone risked eating it. However, I do grow brassicas, some peas and beans, onions, spinach and others together in a vegetable area, partly because neat rows of well-grown crops are in themselves a pleasure to see. They are also one of my most useful teaching subjects. All too often someone fails to recognize onions that are not sliced in rings, or refuses to eat peas from the pod because 'I only eat fresh garden peas from a can.' I regularly work with people for whom a Brussels sprout is a soggy mush that comes frozen in a polythene bag.

Herbs, too, are a constant source of interest and pleasure. A large portion of the garden is devoted to a jumble of herbs growing together. I include artemisia (wormwood), woad, comfrey and others, as well as the more widely used culinary and medicinal herbs. Tall lovage forms a barrier that helps to make this part of the garden something of a secret – there is always a problem in a sloping garden of being able to stand at the top and see it all; a garden should be a series of surprises.

In this respect I was lucky to have a clump of bamboos and a large rhododendron in the field that I started with. These now screen an ornamental pond with its waterfall, lilies, goldfish and waterwheel. This is a peaceful suntrap that provides a home for some tender individuals like bottlebrushes (callistemon), strawberry trees, cordylines and abutilons. The sound of water is soothing to any visitor, but particularly enjoyable for blind and partially sighted people (for whom I have a whole bed of interestingly textured plants too).

The gardens at Churchtown are not necessarily just about pleasant sensations – I grow plants like datura, which is strongly pungent, and ailanthus,

he heavily spined 'devil's walking stick'; plants with interesting names – elephant's ear and lamb's ear; giant pumpkins and tiny, fascinating mouse-plants (arum) which resemble a long-tailed mouse running into its hole, and are pollinated by gnats at night.

Edible plants are always of interest, and as well as the vegetables there is a good range of fruit. Six different cordon apples provide a good example of grafting as well as demonstrating how plants can be adapted to suit a disabled person – cordons can be easily maintained from a wheelchair. When a group of mentally handicapped people, primarily interested in television and the warm indoors, suddenly discover that strawberries come from plants, a whole new incentive and area of interest can quickly develop!

There have been plants that have refused to behave – a fine *Cytisus battandieri* with its rich scent of ripe pineapples, has grown up and well out of the reach of all but the most agile noses. The camomile and thyme lawn is both bald and inaccessible, and if I were to start again I could improve access to many areas of the garden. Part of the aim has always been to involve disabled people in the work of the garden. With perhaps ten disabled people in wheelchairs and only myself and visiting staff it is often hard to provide for the participation I would hope for ideally. An additional problem has been that a throughput of fifty people in a week can demolish a stock of cutting material, or sow an astonishing number of seeds!

There is much to learn from mistakes, and there are many improvements and additions to be made. I was extraordinarily lucky to be able to design a garden at university and then to be invited to build and develop that garden. The product of this is there for all to see. All the plants have been donated or propagated from material fellow gardeners have given to me. Although it is a very personal creation I hope that many more disabled and able-bodied visitors will come and share the pleasures I have enjoyed.

4. The bed containing raspberries and red currants beyond this colourful wigwam of sweet peas runs from nothing to five feet in height so that someone on a stretcher or who cannot bend can enjoy working there.

5. Peter Macfadyen and his staff designed, glazed and built the greenhouse using second-hand timber; here, fifty varieties of fuchsias, mostly from donated cuttings, can withstand unskilled treatment.

Peckover House, Wisbech, Cambridgeshire

GEORGE PEELING, BEM

At first, I did not believe it when the letter arrived from Downing Street; I must have sat and read it a dozen times. I remember my wife asking me, 'What is the matter?' and I said, 'Well, you won't believe it but I'm getting the BEM' – and she couldn't believe it! The trouble was that we had to keep it to ourselves for a month before we could tell anyone and it never really sank in until the Lord Lieutenant of Cambridgeshire gave me the medal at a special ceremony at Peckover House at the beginning of 1984. Having now got over the surprise I realize what an honour it is for a practical man from a working-class family.

I knew Peckover House as a private residence as a boy. My father was a chauffeur-gardener in Wisbech for many years. I can remember him coming home with a handful of cuttings for mother to put in the garden; he put her in that select group of people he believed to have green fingers.

While at school I developed my interest not only in gardening but also in art, and when I left at fourteen I should have become an apprenticed artist with a Wisbech printing works. However, they were only willing to pay one and threepence a week and my parents turned round and said, 'Oh no, you will have to find a little bit better a job than that!' The result was that I became an errand boy at a high-class fishmongers and used to deliver fish to Peckover House for the late Miss Peckover, never realizing at that time of course that I'd land up working here and living in the gardener's house in the garden.

After a year, I left the fishmongers and worked in a local nursery before going into the Royal Air Force at nineteen; after five and a half years of that, much of it in the Far East, I worked on a small nursery and fruit farm in Wisbech for five years and then went on to a larger nursery where bulbs were grown, gaining experience all the time.

On being made redundant by the closing down of the nursery I went into private gardening, but still had two nice greenhouses to care for, growing pot plants, toms, cues and chrysanths for my employers. I stayed with them for nine years, until I heard about the job which was going at Peckover.

At first I thought there must be something wrong about this as the National Trust seemed to have had two gardeners in a very short time. Nevertheless, I applied for the job; I can still remember my interview because of one particular question asked by the then Regional Agent of the Trust. 'Are you honest?' he said. I was rather taken aback by this and it took me a minute or two to wonder what I should say. On being pressed I told him, 'The best thing you can do is to get in touch with my employer.' He was rather surprised but, after he'd done so I was taken on and it was the best thing that ever happened for me.

Although the Peckover garden was like a wilderness I felt at home after a few weeks and could begin to see the results of my efforts; as the days and months went by, I gained increasing satisfaction from it all.

I was soon asked to make two topiary peacocks in the neglected yew hedge, either side of the path to the double borders. When I said that I had never seen a peacock I was told, 'Use your imagination,' and, although I thought they would be out of place in this 2¼-acre garden, I took up the challenge to prove to myself and to others that I could make a reasonable job!

The double borders, designed by Graham Thomas, are laid out so that each border is virtually a mirror of the other. Small hedges of potentillas, *Viburnum opulus* 'Compactum' and *Hydrangea cinerea* 'Sterilis', are used to divide groups of musk roses, fuchsias, santolinas, Japanese anemones, euphorbias, agapanthus and other plants for year-round effect.

Keeping to the original planting plan is not always as easy as you may think because some plants, the anemones for example, are very invasive. The borders are edged with *Dianthus* 'Mrs Sinkins' (or is it 'White Ladies'?). The south garden was originally an orchard and kitchen garden and there is still a very old apple tree in one corner. It is now

1. George Peeling with his favourite fuchsias in the greenhouse.

mostly lawn, with a quince, black mulberry, medlar and Dartmouth crab apple planted in the 1960s. Along the path side there is an informal border of vigorous shrubs, including cotoneasters, lilacs, *rugosa* rosas and a few groups of hardy hebes.

Directly behind the House the area known as the 'Wilderness Walk' reminds me of the shrubbery walks of an old rectory I knew as a young boy. Hollies, laurels, box and yew all grow well and also the spotted laurel (*Aucuba japonica*); we have both male and female forms, so we get lots of scarlet berries in winter. There is a magnificent specimen of *Hydrangea sargentiana*; I have seen nothing to match its size; so far I have not managed to propagate it from cuttings but I will keep trying. Near by are two very old trees: a maidenhair tree (*Gingko biloba*) and a tulip tree (*Liriodendron tulipifera*), perhaps planted by the early Peckover family. Unfortunately, the top blew out of the maidenhair tree in a storm and the tulip tree has recently lost some of its limbs, but replacements have been planted.

The shrubbery lawn has groups of shrubs and trees underplanted with bergenias, alchemillas, hostas, vincas and other ground-cover plants. Visitors are always surprised to see our palm (*Trachycarpus fortunei*) growing in Cambridgeshire; at the foot of the roadside wall, there was once a herbaceous border but it now has a formal pattern of dwarf purple cherry (*Prunus* 'Cistena') with groups of dwarf foliage and flowering plants; I am told it is a Victorian design.

Old climbing roses, clematis and honeysuckles are trained on the garden walls and there are a number of iron arches and pillars in the central part of the garden, also planted with climbing or rambler roses. Some of the roses are now very old and I have propagated several from hardwood cuttings. The 'Bandstand' (well, I call it that because of its shape) has a combination of honeysuckle (*Lonicera etrusca* 'Superba') and a rambler rose 'American Pillar'.

2. Peckover House seen from under the white cherry in the Wilderness Walk.

Most of the roses in the little formal rose garden have just been replanted; 'Margaret Merril' with its terrific scent, the yellow 'Pot o' Gold' and the rich red 'Innoxa Femille' do very well.

Beyond the rose garden and through an iron gate there is a small walled area with a green and white summerhouse, much used by the public, and a small pond surrounded by hydrangeas, buddleias, peonies and lilies.

Probably because I had such a good grounding in it in my early years, greenhouse work is perhaps where I find the most job satisfaction and I think that the display houses are certainly the highlight for the visitors. Nothing too exotic is grown because, through experience, I find people prefer things which they can attempt to grow in their own greenhouses. I have had people tell me how nice the colours of the pot plants look but I don't consciously stage particular plants together; it comes automatically where they should go. Fuchsias do very well and I have propagated some of the cultivars from cuttings given to me by visitors. A few of my favourite varieties are 'Swingtime', 'Moonlight Sonata', 'White Spider', 'Royal Purple' and 'Snow Cap'. Many visitors do not believe that the orange

75

3. The long walk to George Peeling's favourite part of the garden, the greenhouse, is lined with the white *Dianthus* 'Mrs Sinkins'; here in the beds are doronicums, hemerocallis and the white *Viburnum opulus* 'Compactum'.   4. George Peeling's yew peacocks overlook a curved bed of peonies which include the apple-blossom pink 'Sarah Bernhardt'.   5. The 'Bandstand's' unusual planting of *Lonicera etrusca* 'Superba' and the rambler rose 'American Pillar'; in the foreground is white philadelphus.   6. The old-fashioned atmosphere of the rose garden at Peckover is mostly due to these arches of old rose cultivars, interspersed with *Lavandula* 'Hidcote'. The nearest rose is 'Paul's Scarlet Climber'.
7. Behind this formal bed of *Pelargonium* 'Gustav Emich' is a series of four rose arches, the first two of which have 'Crimson Shower' flowering in August; beyond is the light pink 'Dorothy Perkins'.

rees are real and over three hundred
ears old; on occasions I have been
sked, 'Are the fruit plastic?' or 'How
o you thread the oranges on to the
ranches?'

To the side of the Orangery (really a
arge glasshouse) is the lean-to fernery
it; the necessary cool, damp conditions
re helped by the floor being below
round level, although some heat is
equired during the winter months.
One of the best ferns is the staghorn
ern (*Platycerium bifurcatum*), which I
ought for one and sixpence a number
f years ago.

Working at Peckover, I have got used
o dealing with people. At first I tried to
keep out of their way, but they come
nd find you! Even when I am cutting
he grass visitors will stand in the way
nd ask me to stop and explain the name
of a plant or when the maidenhair tree
vas planted or how many other people
work in the garden (none, except for a
part-timer in the summer). Really, I
have few dislikes but I can get annoyed
when fuchsias are broken to get cut-
ings, cigarettes stubbed out on the
greenhouse tiled floor or used tissues
thrown about.

Most days I am out working by 6.30
a.m.: I attend to the greenhouse first
and then walk round the whole garden
to decide what jobs I should tackle.
During the spring and summer months,
when there can be many interruptions,
it can mean going out again after tea to
finish a job. Having been brought up in
the old-fashioned way, I have always
thought that if a job is worth doing it is
worth doing well. As a practical man
I have learned by experience and
not examination qualifications; young
gardeners are encouraged to put too
much store on these nowadays. Fortunately, the National Trust realize that I
am indeed a practical man and when the
Gardens' Adviser, with whom I get on
very well, visits Peckover twice a year
we consider maintenance and any new
developments.

Although there is plenty of colour in
the garden, with many annuals bedded
out each year and the small rose garden,

7.

I have always liked white flowers and
my particular favourite is the white
form of the Japanese wind flower (*Anemone* × *hybrida*). I enjoy propagating
plants; many of the older varieties are
now difficult to obtain – like the geranium *P*. 'Gustav Emich' which I have
managed to increase in numbers. This
was the geranium which for many years
was planted out during the summer
months in front of Buckingham Palace.

My nephew is head gardener at
Grimsthorp Castle, Lincolnshire, and
we visit each other's gardens to exchange plants and discuss the season.
His garden is much bigger than Peck-

over and many vegetables are still
grown for the house. In my own patch I
grow a few vegetables and soft fruit for
my wife and me – not a wide range, just
the usual things like potatoes, lettuces,
carrots, runner beans, raspberries and
strawberries.

My wife, like me, comes from the
Fens and her family were fruit growers
near Wisbech; we have been married
forty-three years and have a daughter
(keen on gardening), a son and three
grandchildren. Retirement, of course,
is not all that far away but when it does
come the sense of fulfilment, especially
at Peckover, will be enormous.

Logan Botanic Garden, Dumfries and Galloway

MARTIN COLLEDGE

People enter the horticultural profession by many doors and I was fortunate in being the son of a head gardener on an estate high on the Lammermuir Hills in the Scottish Border country. This was in pre-war days when country-house gardens were still managed and cultivated to a high standard in the traditional style, and so I became familiar as a boy with what went on in a garden and was taught many of the skills and techniques. I recall still, from long ago, my sense of wonder on being told that the plants being planted one day had been raised from seeds collected in China by a Mr Forrest. Later I found out that they were primulas and discovered the immense contribution that George Forrest had made to our garden flora.

War service was followed by a course at the Royal Botanic Garden, Edinburgh, where my interest in plants was further stimulated and broadened by the vast assemblage of plants available for study. After several years in various jobs I settled at Logan where I have worked for over twenty years, latterly as Assistant Curator. Logan Botanic Garden lies mid-way down the Mull of Galloway, the most southerly point of the Scottish mainland, and it is surrounded by sea on three sides: to the east is the Bay of Luce, to the south and west the Irish Sea and the Atlantic Ocean. Thus the climate is influenced by the Gulf Stream drift and is especially mild in winter, enabling us to cultivate in the open a wide range of plants native to the warm, temperate regions of the world, which normally require glasshouse protection in inland gardens.

In this fourteen-hectare garden hard frost occurs only rarely: −3 or −4°C is considered severe. However, in 1963 and again in 1979 prolonged severe frosts of −12°C and −10°C did occur, decimating the plant collection on both occasions. No deep snow has been seen since 1963 and any which has fallen has been transitory, with no more than 50mm (2 inches) lying for as long as forty-eight hours. The average rainfall is 1,000mm (40 inches) per annum and the soil, varying in its ability to retain moisture, is a light acid loam, shallow in places.

The main weather hazard is wind; frequent gales of up to 50mph blow in from the south-west. In 1984 wind in excess of 80mph blasted the garden and caused considerable damage. These gales, annual events, have, over the years, destroyed most of the original shelter belts; on one occasion thirty trees were blown out overnight, along with shrubs and some of our structural work, and this sort of thing can disrupt our normal work programme for up to six weeks. A normal year's weather at Logan begins with a mild winter with gales and an occasional frost, followed by a cold, dry spring. As we go into summer, periods of drought occur, and then a cool, never too warm, summer is followed by a mild, damp autumn; this is typical of the west coast.

The land, especially in the walled garden which forms the main feature of the Botanic Garden, is historically interesting – in the west wall stands a remnant of Castle Balzieland, the medieval stronghold of the McDoualls of Logan, who lived on this land for centuries. Later generations of this ancient Galloway family were great gardeners; their shell and plant collection was renowned throughout the gardening world.

In 1964 the walled garden and some surrounding woodland was presented by Logan Gardens Trust to the Secretary of State for Scotland to be used as an out-station of the Royal Botanic Garden, Edinburgh. The function delegated to Logan by Edinburgh is to cultivate plants of known wild origin from the southern hemisphere, to be used eventually for scientific study, and to display them to the public in an attractive manner. The plants are usually obtained through seed exchange lists from botanic gardens throughout the world. The seeds are sent to the Edinburgh garden, germinated and grown on there and then, when large enough, they are brought to Logan to be planted out. Keen horticulturalists at home

1. Martin Colledge

Two blue plantings in the water garden: *Geranium grandiflorum* 'Gravetye' and *Meconopsis grandis* 'Springhill'.

lso make valuable contributions.

The task originally given to us by RBG Edinburgh was the conversion of a country-house amenity garden into a garden where large numbers of the public could move freely and comfortably, without getting their feet wet, and be able to see clearly labelled specimens; the needs of disabled visitors had also to be catered for. Renovations involved altering the shapes of lawns and borders, removing old trees, and realigning and draining paths; the plant collection also had to be radically altered to comply with RBG policy.

In carrying out these alterations, we endeavoured to retain as much of the original design as possible, compatible with the demands of a public garden, and many of the fine plants were propagated and replanted.

A ten-year programme was drawn up for the renewal of all services. New staff houses were built, electricity and water supplies renewed, a new access road and car park constructed, a new glasshouse and ancillary buildings erected and a bothy converted into a restaurant. These are all essential requirements for the efficient management of the garden and for the convenience and comfort of staff and visitors.

The most important work done over the years, of great long-term value to the garden, has been the renewal of the shelter belts. Twenty years ago, a belt consisting of a mixture of Corsican and lodgepole pines was planted on the east side. These are now over twenty feet tall, growing rapidly, and are beginning to give some shelter from the searing east winds which blow from January to March. In the original woodland adjacent to the walled garden many of the old trees were removed by felling and many more were blown out by gales. They have been replaced by sycamore, Swedish whitebeam, evergreen oak, common oak, beech and red alder. Use has also been made of two important wind- and salt-resistant shrubs, *Griselinia littoralis* and *Pittosporum tenuifolium*.

We pursue a policy of never destroying natural regeneration of native hardwoods, except where a seedling appears on a site selected for an introduced species. It is wise to thin out natural regeneration judiciously – seedlings from this source make the best trees. In selecting the right species for shelter, one's eye and local experience are the best guides. We look for species which have successfully withstood the rigours and ravages of maritime exposure over a long period, say a hundred years or more.

To the south and west of the original woodland a further ten acres of land was acquired in 1978 and planted with a mixture of hybrid larch, sycamore, spruce and Scots pine; this will provide essential shelter from the wild west winds well into the twenty-first century.

Two groups of plants which quickly catch the eye of the visitor are the tree ferns and cabbage palms. *Cordyline australis*, the New Zealand cabbage palm, common in west-coast gardens, has been cultivated at Logan for a hundred years. In the walled garden there stood from 1913 to 1979, when it was severely damaged by frost and gales, a famous avenue of *C. australis*, composed of sixty-two specimens. In recent years this avenue has been taken out and replanted with young plants raised from seed gathered at Logan. We grow three other species of cordyline: *C. indivisa*, notable in autumn for its violet-

3.

4.

5.

6

3. On an early September morning in the water garden the white, bell-shaped flowers of *Galtonia candicans* contrast with the loose sprays of the purple *Thalictrum dipterocarpum*, with the opening petals of venidio-arctotis in the foreground.   4. Beyond the *Primulae florindae* and the water lilies in Rock Gulley, *Cordyline australis* dominates the skyline with the tree fern *Dicksonia antarctica* beyond.   5. *Watsonia beatricis*.   6. In late summer, this area is filled with a vast collection of Agapanthus Headbourne Hybrids. Here also are other South African species like the orange *Crinum × powellii*.

This very effective plant association in the new garden has alstroemeria, *Filipendula purpurea* and *Anthemis* 'Mrs E. Buxton' alongside the spiny silver leaves of *Onopordon acanthium*.

lue fruits, *C. banksii*, the most attractive species for flower, and *C. pumilio*, dwarf plant resembling a large tuft of cocksfoot grass with arching sprays of small white flowers. *C. australis*, whose white flowers give off an overpowering perfume in midsummer and are followed by white fruits in autumn, regenerates profusely and every year hundreds of seedlings have to be weeded out.

The first of the tree ferns, *Dicksonia antarctica* from south-east Australia, was planted outside in 1912, since when many more have been added. Again, these are plants seen only in the open in mild maritime gardens and never fail to arouse the curiosity of visitors. With their crowns of elegant fronds, dark green in colour, contrasting with their rich, dark brown trunks, they are a majestic sight, especially in the evening twilight.

Another fascinating group of plants worth mentioning is *Echium pininana*, from the Canary Isles; they are related botanically to the forget-me-not. This species is monocarpic: it flowers, sets seed and then dies. It takes three years to grow to flowering size when it pro-

duces a 5–7m spike containing many hundreds of lavender-blue flowers. This is another exotic plant whose cultivation in the open air is confined to very mild gardens and is so much at home at Logan that it self-sows freely.

The most exciting and interesting aspect of botanic garden work is the cultivation of plants collected in the wild. We have been fortunate in the last few years in that we have been able to grow many new species from South Africa and elsewhere, some of which are proving to have good ornamental value. The new and reintroduced species from southern Africa belong to the genera *Sutera*, *Diascia* and *Felicia*. It has to be remembered that not all plants collected in the wild are garden-worthy; many are of use only for scientific research. Others, which might have attractive flowers or foliage, are propagated and planted out for visitors to admire and for horticulturalists to assess their garden potential. The genus *Diascia* is a good example; the species collected so far flower freely in our climate from June to October.

A garden must never stand still, or it dies. There must always be a continuity

of creation and re-creation going on. Plants are not immortal; they flourish, reach a peak and then fade away, even those with a lifespan of a hundred years or more. One skill a gardener must develop is to recognize when the peak is about to be reached and have replacements ready for planting. This is essential, especially with woody plants which deteriorate rapidly with age.

The look of a garden is entirely dependent on the quality of the people who work in it; Logan is fortunate in that today we have a young, competent, hard-working staff – any compliments which are given are due to their effort. The involvement of senior management is also very important, since their encouragement and constructive criticism are valuable and necessary and, most important of all, they authorize the expenditure with which to manage the garden.

My home is a whitewashed stone cottage in the middle of the garden. Views of the garden can be seen from every window; my favourite is from the bedroom, looking out over an avenue of palms. Few gardeners in Britain can equal that.

Mill Cottage, Hitcham, Suffolk

CHRISTOPHER GREY-WILSON

We moved into Mill Cottage in the autumn of 1978. The cottage – built in about 1450 – was run down and the garden, one third of an acre in extent, overgrown and neglected.

One of the first things our new neighbours told us, having quickly learnt that we were keen gardeners, was – 'You won't like the soil, it's Suffolk clay.' However, I soon discovered that our soil broke down nicely and without much effort into a fine tilth in almost all parts of the garden. Suffolk clay abounds in the village and is indeed practically unworkable when wet, while once dried it becomes rock hard and fissured. We are lucky; mainly, I suspect, because the garden has long been cultivated, producing a pleasant friable loam.

It is very tempting, faced with an overgrown garden, to clear the whole lot out and start again. However, I resisted this temptation, for I wanted to see what would appear during the following season. There was a good backbone of mature apple trees, a large 'Blenheim Orange' which is a common variety in Suffolk, an 'Early Worcester' and an 'Ellison's Orange', all laden with fruit during that first autumn. There were three large laburnums, a couple of lilacs, one single, the other double, but both white unfortunately, a fine specimen of *Viburnum carlesii*, almost fifteen feet tall, various other assorted bushes and entanglements of roses in all corners of the garden.

During the first spring clumps of snowdrops, *Galanthus nivalis*, appeared, various daffodils, mats of sweet violets, both violet and white, numerous cowslips and primroses, and a prodigious number of Spanish bluebells, *Endymion hispanicus*, all fine in the cottage garden setting. Most of the climbing roses that sprawled everywhere proved to be the vigorous 'American Pillar', a rather harsh magenta to my eye, so most of these were quickly removed. There was however, a fine 'Albertine', which was pruned and trained to a stout post. Of the shrub roses the only one worth keeping was *Rosa* 'Maxima Alba' with sweetly scented double white flowers set amidst a mass of attractive blue green leaves.

1. In early summer, an arching laburnum frames Mill Cottage and the flower-lined path where alliums, white orris root and irises bloom amongst a profusion of herbaceous plants. *See also page 13*

Christopher Grey-Wilson.

Essentially we wanted a cottage garden with a colourful range of traditional cottage-garden flowers. The English cottage garden is unique in many ways, charmingly rural and totally lacking in formality. In its beginnings it was a practical mixture of vegetables and useful herbs and colourful flowers.

Initially therefore we concentrated on this aspect, working around the backbone of mature trees and bushes. Borders were cut and the lawns relaid. The rather nasty concrete front path was broken up and replaced by a wider, more sympathetic one in hard red bricks, wide enough to allow plants to sprawl across its edges without hindering access. More roses, an essential ingredient in such gardens, were brought in; 'Zéphirine Drouhin' was placed along the front fence, its thornless stems ideal for such a position, and 'New Dawn' was planted against a post to replace one of the 'American Pillar' roses. Shrub roses planted included 'Fantin Latour', 'Frühlingsgold', *Rosa rubrifolia*, for its splendid foliage, *R. mundi*, *R. moyesii* 'Geranium' and *R. rugosa* 'Frau Dagmar Hastrup'. Three smallish trees were planted to provide colour at different seasons, *Prunus sargentii* for its pink spring blossom and striking red autumn colours, *Malus floribunda*, quite one of the best small flowering trees for the average garden and *Robinia pseudoacacia* 'Frisii' for its golden foliage.

The cottage-garden effect was obtained by planting the front borders along the path with a mixture of lavenders and thymes, aubrieta, yellow alyssum and thrift, backed by more robust herbaceous plants. As I am a botanist many other plants quickly crept in, some showy, others more of botanical interest, though I think not distracting from the cottage-garden character. Both my wife, Christine, and I do a lot of illustration, drawing and photographic work, and we need a wide range of plants as subjects.

Gardens on the whole, I feel, have to conform to the prevailing conditions of the area. Suffolk is a relatively dry county, with one of the lowest rainfalls in Britain recorded only ten miles from our cottage. Harsh winters are the norm, but most damaging are the bitter north-east winds. These rush in from the North Sea across the low-lying parts of Norfolk and coastal Suffolk, devastating tender plants and any newly planted shrubs. Shelter is therefore important.

In the autumn of our second year we suffered the traumas of having the roof rethatched. Christine wisely said 'Let's go away on holiday until it's over,' and this we did, returning to a fine new roof, but a flattened and trampled garden. However, it was autumn – most of the herbaceous plants were dying down and most of the bulbous plants were safely below ground in any case.

The front borders face south and in the spring a succession of bulbous plants mix with primroses, cowslips, pretty blue *Omphalodes verna* and the superior and even brighter *O. cappadocica* and *Pulmonaria saccharata* whose handsome large blotched leaves provide interest throughout the summer. Amongst the snowdrops I particularly like *Galanthus ikariae* with its shiny green leaves, *G. nivalis* 'S. Arnott' and *G.* 'Straffan'. These come at the same time as *Crocus tomasinianus* 'Ruby Giant', the winter aconite, *Eranthis hyemalis*, the lovely blue reticulata irises, *Iris reticulata* 'Cantab' and 'J. S. Dijt' and drifts of anemones, *A. blanda*

'Atrocaerulea', 'Radar' and the aptly named 'White Splendour'. Small narcissi provide flowers over many weeks but my own favourites are 'Jack Snipe', 'Dove Wings', 'Tête-à-tête', *Narcissus triandrus* 'Thalia' and *N. jonquilla* 'Baby Moon'. Bulbs do very well in Suffolk gardens, especially on the lighter soils, aided by the low rainfalls and bright summers. Coarser types succeed, like the bold clumps of crown imperials, *Fritillaria imperialis*, both red and yellow forms, the very striking *F. persica* 'Adiyaman', and the smaller species, *F. meleagris*, *F. uva-vulpis* and the strong-smelling *F. pyrenaica*. Juno irises thrive in the light soil. Both *Iris orchioides*, with its bright yellow flowers, and *I. magnifica*, pale blue and white forms, increase slowly, and even the rare *I. cycloglossa* from Afghanistan survives outdoors, producing one or two delicate blue blooms each June.

Midsummer in the front garden is marked by a succession of colourful perennials. Hardy geraniums, *G. ibericum*, *G. endressii*, *G. psilostemon* with its vivid purple flowers, the widely grown *G.* 'Johnson's Blue' and the surprisingly little seen *G. pratense* 'Rectum Album', all vie with each other in a medley of colour. Bold masses of oriental poppies, *Papaver orientalis* 'Goliath' and 'Cedric's Pink' are guaranteed to attract attention, though sadly they provide only a fleeting show. An old cottage-garden favourite *Hesperis matronalis* 'Alba' (dames violet), with its sweetly-scented rocket flowers, is attractive to orange-tip butterflies. *Anchusa* 'Loddon Royalist' is a splendid plant, a little untidy, but quite one of the best blues in the summer garden. Later, the gaps vacated by the oriental poppies are filled by *Campanula lactiflora* 'Loddon Anna', with its subtle pale pink flowers, and bright yellow *Anthemis sancti-johannis*, and these provide colour throughout July and August. In the front of the border *Campanula × burghaltii* drips its splendid grey-blue bells in profusion, short-lived but quite delightful. Here also, tufts of brilliant blue *Tradescantia*

83

virginiana 'Isis' contrast with rose clusters of *Stachys macrantha*.

A succession of ornamental onions push through the summer perennials from June onwards. I am particularly fond of these for they are delightful in flower, and later they make very useful dried decorations. *Allium afflatunense* and the striking *A. christophii* with its huge loose balls of metallic-purple starry flowers are the finest. Both are easy to grow. Another favourite is *Allium siculum*, elegant with its relatively large greenish bells. Of the smaller, the most appealing for me are *A. flavum, A. pulchellum* and *A. karataviense*, with its handsome broad-ribbed leaves and dense heads of whitish-pink flowers.

The autumn is not forgotten in the garden. By the time *Prunus sargentii* has changed from green to vivid crimson and the roses, *R. moyesii* and *R. rugosa*, are dripping with waxy red hips, the autumn flowers are opening. Patches of *Cyclamen hederifolium*, both pink and white, and the daintier *C. cilicium* find places below shrubs and mix with the brilliant sealing-wax red berries of *Arum italicum* 'Pictum'. Colchicums sprout beneath the apple tree in the front garden, *C. speciosum* and its splendid white form 'Album' bear their large goblet flowers over several weeks, together with the chequered flowers of *C. bivonae* (= *C. bowlesianum*) and the slighter *C. autumnale*, the so called 'autumn crocus'. However, the true autumn crocuses – *Crocus speciosus* and *C. pulchellus* – are also present.

I had not originally planned to have a scree garden despite a life-long love of alpine plants. However, there were heaps of nasty rubble in the garden when we arrived and it seemed a pity not to take advantage of it. I dug a deep broad pit about three feet deep and placed two feet of rubble in the bottom, followed by a layer of inverted turves, with a gritty peaty loam mixture filling the top nine inches. I decided that a raised bed would be out of keeping with the overall cottage-garden effect, so the

3.

84

5.

6.

3. Chris Grey-Wilson's scree garden has many small alpine species flowering during May and June: *Anemone magellanica* (cream) contrasts with the deep blue *Lithospermum diffusum* and with pink *Erinus alpinus*. 4. From the cottage, ox-eye daisies and *Allium afflatunense* vie with the yellow *Piptanthus nepalensis*. 5. A lush growth of irises, hostas and alchemilla masks the edge of the pond. Bright pink *Phuopsis stylosa* and thymes creep over the retaining wall.
6. *Arisaema griffithii*, found in the Himalayas, has a bizarre flowerhead like a brooding cobra.

surface of the scree was finished off with a covering of coarse grit and strategically placed rocks at lawn level, the edge being bounded by a ring of old red bricks cemented into place to stop the lawn invading the scree. The scree has proved highly successful. In the spring patches of *Iris reticulata* 'Cantab' and *Narcissus bulbocodium* bring a sudden burst of colour. They are soon followed by pink patches of *Erinus alpinus* and several different free-flowering clones of the dazzling blue *Gentiana acaulis*, guaranteed to attract attention. Patches of pink moss campion, *Silene acaulis*, one of the loveliest of British native species, attract the spring butterflies and flower at the same time as *Iris lutescens* (*I. chamaeiris*) and *Primula marginata* with its mealy-edged leaves and deep pink primrose flowers. During the summer coarser plants come into flower. *Euryops acraeus*, its yellow flowers set amidst a filigree of silvery-grey leaves, vies with the deep blue bristly hummocks of *Leptospermum diffusum* and pink and white *Onosma albo-rosea*. In the autumn *Leucojum autumnale*, a dainty white and pink snowflake and the popular *Gentiana sino-ornata*, given a peaty hollow, complete the season.

We are both keen to encourage wildlife into the garden. Bird-boxes are placed on convenient trees and under the eaves and a wide selection of scented and aromatic herbs attract a myriad of bees and butterflies. Chemical sprays are kept to the minimum and used with care and discretion.

The pond, dug out of the front lawn, is one of our favourite spots. The shape is informal and the margins thickly planted with a tangled mass of water forget-me-not, *Myosotis aquatica*, musk, *Mimulus guttatus*, and cotton-grass, *Eriophorum angustifolium*. In the spring, bright yellow marsh marigolds, *Caltha palustris* 'Flore Plena', are the first to flower. At midsummer our native flowering rush, *Butomus umbellatus*, comes into flower, though it does not do so every year. Irises include *I. pseudacorus*, the native yellow

flag, *I. laevigata* 'Variegata' and *I. kaempferi*, set amidst robust stems of giant buttercups, *Ranunculus lingua*.

On the north end of the cottage a permanently shaded area of garden has given me a chance to construct a small peat garden, using peat blocks as a basis. Such gardens are not ideal in Suffolk because of the dry climate, but plants have succeeded well enough. In the spring *Uvularia perfoliata* drips its yellowed flared flowers and the bloodroot, *Sanguinaria canadensis* 'Flore Plena', mixes with tufts of *Primula gracilipes* from Nepal, *P. rosea* and deep pink *Cortusa matthiola*. My favourite plants on the peat are the arisaemas, aristocratic arums; the best by far is *A. sikokianum* from Japan. Here in the dappled shade our rarest native orchid, *Cypripedium calceolus*, lives a solitary existence, flowering occasionally, but never multiplying, an aggravating beauty.

To me the greatest joy of being a botanist is to be able to observe plants growing in the wild, and I have been fortunate to have been on a number of botanical expeditions, primarily in Afghanistan, Nepal and East Africa. On these expeditions I always keep an eye open for a potentially good garden plant and some find their way, if hardy, into my own garden.

Gardens mature over a number of years, and I never expect initial plantings to be in any way a final scheme. I frequently walk around the garden just to look and see if particular plants would fit better in another location, or in a different association. It is so much easier to see planting schemes when looking at plants in flower, than trying to visualize plantings on a piece of paper. One can only really know how particular plants will succeed in a garden by growing them. So in my garden plants are moved around until I am satisfied that they could not be better placed.

A neighbour leaned over the front fence just a short while ago and looked slowly over the garden from left to right – 'You be bringing it round all right then,' he said.

Castle Howard, Yorkshire

BRIAN HUTCHINSON

In 1967 Christopher Hussey wrote in *English Gardens and Landscapes:* 'The environs of Castle Howard can still be called, in Horace Walpole's words, "the grandest scenes of rural magnificence" that were created in the eighteenth century. "Nobody told me . . . that I should at one view see a palace, a town, a fortified city, temples on high places, woods worthy of being each a metropolis of the Druids, the noblest lawn in the world fenced by half the horizon, and a mausoleum that would tempt one to be buried alive."'

The first approach to an estate such as Castle Howard gives one an immediate and lasting impression; for myself the initial impact was made by the avenues of beech and lime stretching in a straight line for five miles, with, almost at the halfway mark, the obelisk commemorating the work of Charles Howard, 3rd Earl of Carlisle (1669–1738).

The gardens were neglected during the last war, and during the 1950s and 1960s much clearing and reclaiming had to be done. There were some plantings of rhododendrons, azaleas, shrubs and ornamental trees and large plantings of daffodils. Wherever suitable spaces become available more daffodils are planted. In the spring the grounds are a remarkable sight, with some less common varieties spreading the daffodil season over a period of some six weeks. Other notable features are the large expanse of fine lawns, the yew hedges and the specimen trees. During the mid 1970s we planted quite large collections of betula, sorbus and amelanchier, and these are now beginning to make their mark on the landscape.

It is with the more recent changes that I am mostly involved; through the vision of the late Lord Howard we embarked on a series of developments commencing in 1975. Plans were laid for new gardens within the walls of the kitchen garden (or market garden). The first to be laid was in the centre section on the eastern side, known as Lady Cecilia's Garden, dedicated to the memory of Lord Howard's wife, who died in 1974. The designs for this and those that followed were made by James Russell, a life-long friend of Lord Howard, who had previously owned Sunningdale Nurseries in Surrey. Most of the planting was undertaken between the autumn of 1975 and the spring of 1976. This particular section is one and a quarter acres, previously used for market-garden crops, and no doubt this was reflected in the good growth we achieved in the early years.

Lady Cecilia's garden is centred on Gardener's House and is essentially a garden of old roses with appropriate inter- and under-planting. The collection began with the purchase of as many varieties of old rose as possible; but since then many more have been discovered, either abroad (and brought back as bud wood) or from other gardens in this country. Unfortunately these roses only flower once and their colour range is limited, there being no reds or yellows. The layout of this garden is designed to accommodate and show off the old varieties, whose growth is generally strong and sprawling. The side walks have trellis frames eight feet high on which roses are trained; yews, planted as two-foot specimens in 1975, have reached the height of the trellis and have now been topped.

Albas, damasks, centifolias and their mossy sports are all old roses, and each has its own peculiarity and fascination;

1. Brian Hutchinson.

86

2. One of the Long Walks in Lady Cecilia's Garden.

the colour range includes whites, pinks, mauves and purples, and most of them are scented. Some are rather prone to mildew and black spot, depending on season and locality. I myself find the other plants in this garden as interesting and important as the roses; the low clipped box hedging contrasting with the pleached hornbeam that frames the house when you first enter the garden, the lime arbours and hornbeam archways. The under-planting is an essential ingredient, providing a blend of appropriate colours, forms and textures and extending the season, particularly after the roses are over. Here we have used large quantities of dianthus, phlox, sages, salvias, geraniums, peonies, thymes, lavenders, silver foliage subjects, sedums, hostas and fuchsias, to name only a few. As well as roses on the surrounding walls, we have ceanothus, choisya, jasmine, honeysuckles and, of course, clematis, including three of my favourites – *Clematis alpina* 'White Moth', 'Perle d'Azur' and 'Comtesse de Bouchaud'.

Going through the hornbeam archway towards the Satyr Gate we enter an area of more modern roses. To the west of the central path is the Sundial Garden, with a collection of over ninety varieties of hybrid tea and floribunda roses planted in 1978. The individual beds are edged with pansies or violas, a particular favourite of Lord Howard. It is possible to leave the same plants in for at least two years, provided they are cut back hard at the end of August so that they build up a good crown before the onset of winter. They then flower earlier the following year. These beds are enclosed by yew hedges; eventually we intend to establish archways in yew to lead from one section to another.

To the east of this is the Venus Garden, started in 1980, which contains the makings of a collection of hybrid perpetual roses. The colours of these roses are basically red, quite a contrast to those in Lady Cecilia's garden. Here the borders are edged with hebe and fuchsias. This garden is surrounded on two sides by yew hedging and on the other two by an oak pergola. This will eventually be clothed with roses and honeysuckle. In this section a long wall border facing south contains the makings of a collection of tea roses, China roses, hybrid musks and modern shrub roses, with some inter-planting of liliums, agapanthus, galtonia and alliums.

The development over a few years of these three rose gardens has involved over two and a half acres of intensive planting. To complete the scene I should mention two fairly extensive borders of hardy fuchsias. The borders are both north-facing and come into their own in late summer. In addition, facing west, there is a fifty-yard-long border of delphiniums, all of the Blackmore and Langdon strain, edged and inter-planted with annuals and perennials with white, pink or blue flowers to provide interest after the delphiniums have faded. Two twenty-five-yard borders complete the scene; here we 'bed out' twice a year with colourful subjects.

While the rose gardens are the centre of attraction, and rightly so, Lord Howard was also keen to develop other areas of the grounds and work continued apace with the creation of an ornamental woodland garden in the adjoining Wray Wood. The garden contains a large collection of rhododendrons and azaleas, unusual trees, rare shrubs and ground cover; planting is now almost complete and the area has been opened to the public. It is hard to believe that it once contained close-planted hardwoods, with almost solid ground cover of brambles and laid timber thinnings. The next venture is to go into the parkland and develop a very extensive arboretum, but this is, of course, a very long-term project.

The final addition is a plant centre, laid out in 1981, where the public can buy plants, including some that may be difficult to obtain elsewhere.

On leaving school I entered gardening as a second-best occupation – my first choice was to be a carpenter – but

3.

en in those days some jobs were not
sy to find. I suppose gardening was
ot an unreasonable choice, as my
ther was a keen exhibitor of flowers
d vegetables. My early days were
ent in the gardens and greenhouses at
hatsworth, getting the basic ground-
g. After five years I took a full-time
urse in commercial horticulture, and
en returned to Chatsworth, where I
ayed until 1965. My interest in educa-
on had been developing for some time,
d so in 1965 I was fortunate enough
become head gardener at the
ottinghamshire College of Agricul-
re, with a staff of five. All aspects of
ardening were covered and, with re-
lanting and new developments, I en-
yed my time there immensely. But
r some time I had been uneasy about
orking for the 'local authority', as it
ere, so I went back to the system I had
en brought up to, the private estate –
ence my arrival at Castle Howard in
973.

After two years in Yorkshire I still
ad not made any contact with other
rofessional gardeners; I had attended
roup meetings at Harlow Car regular-
y, but on these occasions met only the
een amateur, so in 1976 I contacted
everal other head gardeners from pri-
ate gardens in Yorkshire with a view to
orming some organization for the pro-
essional in private gardens. I had every
ncouragement from Lord Howard
rom the outset. After several months
f exploratory talks, the Professional
Gardeners' Guild was founded, and we
ave managed to bring together many
ardeners who would otherwise be
perating in isolation. We visit each
ther's gardens and the discussions and
ontacts are particularly valuable for
he younger gardeners.

The success of large private gardens
epends upon the cooperative efforts
f owners and gardeners. There is
remendous public interest in plants
nd gardens at present, and I believe
hat gardens such as the one at Castle
Howard will continue to give pleasure
or many years to come.

4.

5.

3. *Cedrus atlantica glauca* frames Castle
Howard, with drifts of early-flowering daffodils
in the foreground.   4. In Lady Cecilia's Garden,
the hybrid musk rose 'Felicia' stands out from a
mass planting of *Campanula lactiflora*.   5. Pink
Rosa gallica 'Complicata' and white *Rosa
centiflora* 'Blanchefleur' bloom freely inside the
east wall hand gate.   6. The Vanbrugh-designed
Gardener's House overlooks Lady Cecilia's
Garden, including this bed of pink
'Lavender Lassie' and purple 'Chianti' shrub
roses.

6.

The Dorothy Clive Garden, Willoughbridge Garden Trust, Market Drayton, Shropshire

GEORGE LOVATT

The Dorothy Clive garden, nestling in idyllic countryside on the Staffordshire–Shropshire border, is a seven-acre memorial garden to the wife of Colonel Harry Clive, who founded the Willoughbridge Garden Trust in 1958, five years before he died.

Until I started work on the garden, in June 1968, it had been known primarily for its spring blaze of colour, mainly due to the old gravel quarry planted with rhododendrons and azaleas, one of the most comprehensive collections in the Midlands region.

However, the rest of the garden – some three and half acres of planted banks of bulldozed soil, with just a collection of trees for shelter – was almost aching with unfulfilled potential. I sensed immediately that this was a unique, once-in-a-lifetime opportunity to create a garden, my chance to put some of the ideas from my early training into effect.

I had trained with Bill Harris, head gardener at Betton House, near Market Drayton, and then spent some time at the world-famous Abbey Gardens, Tresco. It was Bill, an enthusiastic follower of Gertrude Jekyll's idea of 'painting' with plantings, who had first instilled in me the feeling for views through gardens and the idea of using collections of plants together to create impressions.

It was in 1972, following the appointment of a local enthusiast, Dr Charles Catlin, as honorary curator, that work on the construction of the extension of the garden really got under way. In the early days the freelance landscape gardener, John Codrington, was called in to help with the initial plans for the redevelopment of the garden. We set about converting the whole area into a seven-acre all-interest garden to attract visitors throughout the spring, summer and autumn months.

I soon realized that there was considerable scope for the construction of a pool and for a scree leading up from the water-garden to provide an interesting area of alpine plants.

The making of a pool on the site of an old sandpit at the bottom of the south-facing bank was of course a major job, especially as I was undertaking the work with the help of only one assistant. It was exciting though, instructing the bulldozer inch by inch to carve out the pool, about thirty feet by eighteen feet, and to build up a dam to stop at last the wholesale leakage of top soil on to the main road. (I had spent many a morning-after-the-storm shovelling silt from the highway!)

The edges of the pool were blurred

1. George Lovatt in the rock garden.

The scree garden in June.

with a wide-ranging collection of aquatic plants and marginal material. Soon ornamental grasses, primulas, irises and many other water-loving specimens like *Dierama pulcherrimum*, the wand flower, were flourishing.

The scree was another challenge, and one that I was to relish. First it had to be drained to catch and disperse the water which gushed from the tops of the banks. The acid sandy soil was in dire need of humus, which we added, mainly in the form of leafmould. The enriched soil, topped with gravel, was to provide the almost perfect environment for the alpines, helping to conserve the moisture in the summer months but keeping the necks of the plants dry and so enabling them to survive the English winter.

The combination of this water-garden and scree is one of the most photographed pieces of gardening work in the Midlands. Whenever I sit on the seat at the bottom of the scree looking up at one of the focal points, such as the *Ilex aquifolium* 'Flavescens', I think how fortunate I was to have had the opportunity to create such a scene.

The scree was built in such a way that visitors can walk around the gravel-covered surface in search of their favourite plants. The choice is varied, with wide selections of thymes, saxifrages, sempervivums and hypericums amongst dwarf willows, conifers and delicate Japanese maples. Particularly noteworthy are *Celmisia spectabilis*, androsaces and the South African shrub, *Euryops evansii*. The whole project took some considerable time to complete, being designed and planted for easy maintenance – and done on a shoestring, too.

Near the bungalows at the top of the garden I introduced a long stone retaining wall, built with stone from a ha-ha on a nearby estate. Two inmates from a local open prison helped me to complete it. In the bed on top of the retaining wall I have planted a wide range of sun-loving plants backed up by varieties of *Pinus mugo*, junipers and various conifers.

The very feature that had made the garden popular in the first place, the old gravel quarry, was in need of considerable attention. The paths had to be widened and considerable pruning was necessary to bring the extensive collection of rhododendrons and azaleas back under control.

Throughout the construction of the garden I have planned many cross-garden views taking in contrasting areas – the pond, the scree, the retaining wall and the woodland. We are fortunate at Willoughbridge in having lovely rolling countryside around the garden, almost as if Capability Brown had created the surrounding area to complement the garden.

3.

4.

In my training emphasis was given t
the need to concentrate on plants tha
could easily be sustained on the type c
soil and conditions available; here a
Willoughbridge the cistus do excep
tionally well, as do the hebes, shrubb
penstemons and daphnes. In th
woodland areas the hostas, lilies an
hydrangeas are a feature.

Now that the garden has settled int
an early maturity it is at a crucial stag
in its development; there is a need t
insert new plants and replace some o
the shrubs which are getting old and
little woody.

In recent years I have met some o
the top gardeners in Britain and it ha
been a particular pleasure to welcom
many of them to Willoughbridge.
have been touched and inspired by thei
encouragement and their interes
in a garden I have enjoyed develop
ing and maintaining this last sixteer
years.

. George Lovatt encourages the jungle effect
produced by these Exbury and Knaphill hybrid
azaleas, flourishing in the old quarry.   4. The
rock garden and sloping scree rise behind the
pond. This is planted with moisture-loving
things like primulas, hostas, cornus, willows and
the striking *Glyceria aquatilis* 'Variegata'.
5. *Romneya coulteri*, growing in a hot, sandy
spot above the rock garden.   6. The low
early-morning sun in the old quarry highlights a
fine specimen of Ghent azalea 'Nancy Waterer'
by a group of 'Pink Pearl' rhododendrons.
7. An autumn afternoon shows the natural effect
achieved by the use of a stone and cobbled path
linking pond and rock gardens.

7.

Clapton Court Gardens, Crewkerne, Somerset

BOB BARNES

The gardens at Clapton Court in Somerset were first opened to the public by Captain Loder in 1979, but it was not until March 1981 that I was appointed head gardener and moved, with my family, from a small Cotswold estate into the head gardener's cottage at Clapton.

I have a typical cottage garden, crammed to overflowing with hundreds of plants for year-round colour and interest. This complements, and contrasts with, the spacious gardens surrounding the big house. These are divided effectively into separate 'rooms', which include three bordered terraces, the rose garden, rockery, formal and informal water gardens and a spring garden. All are simply and elegantly planted, interspersed with open sweeping lawns. Beyond the 'ha-ha' lies the Woodland Garden.

Our stone-built cottage faces south and the garden is sheltered from the north and east winds by a high hedge, thus making an ideal site for the raised beds and rock gardens which surround two small pools. The different parts of the garden are joined by gravel paths; regular raking keeps these in good condition and stops young weed seedlings from getting hold.

The garden is not exactly planned; I love collecting plants that take my fancy, and any new ones are squeezed in between established ones, the overall effect being to create bold splashes of colour from flowers and foliage – a deliberate kaleidoscope. *Regale* lilies grow between roses and escallonia, which is cut back hard each year lest it swamps the roses; clumps of white astilbe mingle with tall yellow irises on the edge of a goldfish pool; half-hardy fuchsias fill every available bare corner round the cottage and I have quite a collection of hardy fuchsias which remain in the ground all winter.

I am not fond of empty wall space; that is why the front of the cottage is becoming covered with climbers and shrubs which need wall protection. These include *Campsis radicans*, with trumpet-shaped flowers of bright yellow and red, which flourishes on this warm, sunny wall; *Abutilon megapotamicum*, which produces red and yellow bell-shaped blooms through summer and early autumn; wistaria, evergreen ceanothus and the super, white-flowered *Clematis* 'Marie Boisselot'. *Colutea arborescens*, the bladder senna, with yellow pea flowers, is also planted here for shelter, along with the shrubby yellow calceolaria and caryopteris, which is covered with hundreds of tiny blue flowers in the late summer and early autumn.

Of the great variety of plants I collect, my first love must be the slow-growing and dwarf conifers, especially those with yellow foliage. There are many new varieties, but I still grow old favourites like *Thuja occidentalis* 'Rheingold'. It is a reliable plant, keeping its colour all through the winter, but in May it looks splendid as the bright yellow new growths appear.

Judging by the number of questions I get asked about them, many people do not seem to realize just how big some of the dwarf conifers grow and wonder how they are going to keep them a reasonable size for the small garden. Surprisingly, a tiny, well-grown plant of *Thuja* 'Rheingold' about six inches tall will get to three or four feet in si[x] years, smothering smaller nearb[y] plants if sited in a small rockery.

The best way to control conifers o[f] this type is to clip or prune them int[o] the required size or shape in April eac[h] year or, if you really want to restric[t] growth for a year, be ruthless and tr[y] root-pruning. This is done by choppin[g] through all the roots with a spade in [a] circle twelve inches away from the mai[n] stem, not forgetting that the root[s] underneath need to be cut as well.

Other conifers include *Juniperus vir[-] giniana* 'Skyrocket', a thin columna[r] tree with blue-grey foliage. There ar[e] also *Chamaecyparis pisifera* 'Boule[-] vard' (whose young shoots are a mar[-] vellous silvery blue), *Chamaecypari[s] lawsoniana* 'Pembury Blue' (easily th[e] best blue in my opinion; it needs plent[y] of room though, as it reaches a height o[f] thirty feet or more) and *Juniperu[s] squamata* 'Blue Star' (a very good blu[e] semi-prostrate juniper). I have trie[d] both *Chamaecyparis pisifera* 'Snow['] and *Juniperus communis* 'Depress[a] Aurea' without much success; th[e] young shoots always seem to die bac[k] during either very wet or very col[d] weather, so both should be planted in [a] sunny, sheltered spot to be seen at thei[r] best.

Between the conifers I have plante[d] heathers, dwarf hebes, small sprin[g] bulbs and the beautiful hardy cyclame[n] – *C. neapolitanum* for autumn flower[-] ing, *C. coum* for winter and *C. repan[-] dum* for spring; all have most attractiv[e] leaves, often with striking marble[d] patterns.

After conifers, pelargoniums (th[e] non-hardy geraniums) are my secon[d]

. Bob Barnes working near the entrance to the Woodland Garden at Clapton Court.

choice of plant; I bed them out in my garden for non-stop summer flowering. The ivy-leafed varieties associate well with the mellow stone on the rockery and I usually plant such varieties as 'Lilac Gem', which has attractive pale mauve blooms, 'Madame Crousse', a mass of pink flowers for many months, or 'L'Elegante', whose white flowers have mauve veins; its striking variegated leaves are cream, dark green and sometimes purple – a very handsome plant.

We specialize in pelargoniums at Clapton Court. Many of them are planted out in urns and ceramic pots in the gardens; 'Red Mini Cascade' and 'Rose Mini Cascade', excellent varieties for this purpose, are both free-flowering dwarf ivy-leafed plants with narrow-petalled flowers.

We raise hundreds of pelargoniums from cuttings for sale in the Glasshouse; cuttings can be taken at any time of the year, even without a greenhouse. Put the plant in a warm place, perhaps on the kitchen window-sill, but out of

direct sunlight, and make sure that the medium you use to put the cuttings in, whether sand, peat or compost, does not get over-watered. They root far better in dry soil, even with the leaves drooping sometimes, as many cuttings are lost by rotting off if the soil is too damp. The quickest results are from cuttings taken in April, which root within a couple of weeks; pinch out the top of the cutting as soon as it has rooted and you should have a good bushy plant within six weeks.

The planning of the mixed borders in the formal garden here is done by Captain and Mrs Loder and they have demonstrated what can be achieved by planting one-colour beds. The first and second terraces feature plants with silver and grey foliage and white flowers, while the top terrace has a spectacular border of predominantly yellow flowers or yellow foliage.

The Woodland Garden at Clapton is one of the most exciting, unusual and interesting parts. Mature trees make an ideal canopy of light shade for the

numerous varieties of camellias, rhododendrons, magnolias and many other rare shrubs. We have the biggest and probably the oldest common ash, *Excelsior fraxinus*, on the mainland of Great Britain and a very fine *Metasequoia glyptostroboides* planted from the original seed brought from China.

With so many interesting and unusual plants and shrubs in the gardens, there is a big demand for plants to buy. Soon after coming here, I reorganized the stock beds and propagation unit so as to provide what the visitors want. As well as the open stock beds, I have net tunnels for the plants which might be affected by the winter winds and frost, like young ceanothus, abutilons and jasminums.

There are not too many occupations where a man's work is also his hobby. Gardening is one, and I have always appreciated that. Coming home to my own cottage garden provides me with as much creative relaxation, by contrast, as any professional could want.

95

2. One of two pools in Bob Barnes's garden; this one is planted around with dianthus, thrift, variegated grasses (phalaris), hebe, campanula and *Festuca glauca*. 3. Bob Barnes's cottage, hung with *Wistaria sinensis* and the white *Clematis* 'Marie Boisselot' stands in a garden full of plants, including the *alba* rose 'Céleste' and the white lily 'Limelight'. 4. The cottage path overflows with pink and white candytuft and *Calceolaria integrifolia*. On the wall bloom the brilliant red calyces of *Abutilon megapotamicum* with their 'skirt' of yellow petals. 5. This idyllic Somerset scene at Clapton Court looks beyond the ha-ha towards the Woodland Garden from under a fine specimen of *Aesculus flava*.

3.

Bodnant Garden, Tal-y-Cafn, Colwyn Bay, Clwyd

MARTIN R. PUDDLE

Bodnant Garden, where I grew up, is situated on the east bank of the River Conwy and overlooks part of the Snowdon range of mountains. It begins with the natural advantage of abundant running water and a background of large native trees, some of them planted in the late eighteenth century. It now appears as a garden of grand vistas and dramatic effects but you will discover that there are more intimate areas as well.

The present Lord Aberconway's great-grandfather, Henry Pochin, bought the estate in 1875: at that period only a small garden existed, near the house, but other features were soon added and he planted many of the large trees which are at their prime in the Dell today. During his time the famous Laburnum Arch was created and continues to be a great feature of the garden when at its best in late May and early June.

On Mr Pochin's death the garden passed to his daughter Laura, who became the first Lady Aberconway. She entrusted the garden to her son, Henry Duncan, who had shown great interest in it at an early age and it was he who made Bodnant as we know it today. From 1903 the garden developed rapidly under his great care and creative skill.

This gentleman, the second Lord Aberconway, was not only a good designer but a brilliant gardener and devoted all the time his many business activities would allow to Bodnant. He designed the six grand terraces which progress down from the house towards the river and he also helped to finance many plant-hunting expeditions to China, the Himalayas, Chile, Tasmania

and other temperate regions. Bodnant was thus enriched by a great wealth of new plants, many of which proved to be of great garden merit.

His son, the present Lord Aberconway, is as keenly interested in Bodnant as was his father and has managed the garden with equal skill and devotion. Until his recent retirement he was, like his father, President of the Royal Horticultural Society for over twenty years.

As a young boy in 1920, Lord Aberconway was writing a birthday 'thank you' letter to his godmother Miss Ellen Willmott, still regarded as one of the greatest woman gardeners and plantswomen of all time. Having difficulty in filling the page he mentioned that the head gardener had died and that his father was looking for a replacement. Miss Willmott wrote back to ask if this were true and, if so, to recommend my grandfather, Frederick Charles Puddle, then head gardener at Scampston Hall, Yorkshire.

Frederick and his employer worked together on the rapid development and planning of the garden. My grandfather was also responsible for raising seedlings from seeds sent back by the plant-hunting expeditions between the two world wars. He had become interested in hybridization when working with orchids at Scampston and was soon using his skills in producing new rhododendrons and other plants.

Thousands of seedlings were grown in pans and pots, both species and new young hybrids, in small wooden greenhouses. They were then potted into small containers and grown on inside so that flowers were forced. Continuous selection took place and any weak plants

were discarded – those which were no good in flower colour, form or size, or foliage. More and more crosses were made over a period of many years and only the best were chosen for further propagation. This process continued and resulted in the raising of numerous rhododendron hybrids which are well known today. *R. griersonianum* was often used as one of the parents and these hybrids became known as Bodnant Reds. Many hybrids won high awards when exhibited in London, including 'Elizabeth', 'Choremia', 'Matador' and 'Siren'. It must have been a most interesting and rewarding time.

On Frederick's retirement in 1947 my father Charles took over the numerous responsibilities which go into administering a garden of this size. The rhododendron hybridization continued but was now concentrated on dwarf, compact, free-flowering plants; plant expeditions were supported (and still continue to be). Extensive planting took

1. Martin Puddle at Pin Mill on the Canal Terrace, with *Yucca filamentosa*.

ace and new areas were developed; ill and imagination were used to reate new vistas and the collection plants was continually increased to reate interest at all times of the year.

In 1949 the garden was given to the ational Trust and during my father's me the number of visitors rose at a emendous rate and continuous imovements had to be made to cope; day we welcome as many as 135,000 a ar.

My father retired in November 1982 d I was invited by Lord Aberconway d the National Trust to succeed him head gardener. It was a great honour be asked to supervise and administer arge garden with such a tremendous putation and one which I have always garded as home. To follow my father d grandfather was a daunting task but ooked upon it as a great opportunity d challenge.

I did not have long to wait for the first allenge; the winter of 1981/2 had a vastating effect on our vast collection plants. Very low temperatures for n days, accompanied by gale-force inds, proved too much for thousands mature plants, including rho-dendrons, wall shrubs and even ses, all of which had survived the evious hard winters of 1947 and 1963. eplanting schemes were begun imediately and continue to the present that, with hard work by our loyal aff, considerable progress has been ade towards returning the garden to s former glory. Many alterations are ogressing and, at the same time, paths ve been widened to take small achinery without, I hope, spoiling the anquil surroundings.

Bodnant is open to the public from id-March to the end of October and I n constantly asked when is the best me to visit. The reply is that you must sit the garden at least three times a ear to appreciate its full beauty. In larch the early-flowering shrubs and affodils are normally at their best and uring April the rhododendrons, mag-olias, cherries and camellias come into eir own. May and June see the climax

2. Evergreen azaleas near 'The Bath' in front of Bodnant Hall in May.

of the rhododendrons and the brilliant colours of the deciduous and Japanese azaleas forming a carpet beneath the natural oaks. The Chilean firebush, *Embothrium lanceolatum*, of which we have several specimens, their long branches clothed with scarlet tubular flowers, do well in our acid soil and in sheltered sites. *Pieris formosa forrestii* 'Wakehurst' has lovely white racemes of lily-of-the-valley-type flowers, followed by brilliant young scarlet growths. On the terraces, the early herbaceous plants and the wall shrubs flower at this time but the lewisias from the Rocky Mountains are one of the star attractions, thriving in the drystone walls.

The terrace gardens are at their best in July and August when the long herbaceous borders, rose beds and water lilies are most colourful. Much space is given to the genus *Clematis* and many species and garden forms are trained against the walls and pergolas at the end of the lower rose terrace. Amongst the many wall plants are *Pileostegia viburnoides*, an evergreen self-clinging climber from southern China, *Clerodendrum bungei*, with deep pink corymbs, and *Hydrangea* 'Blue Wave'

with its large lace-cap flowers. This, with other hydrangeas, provides a bold display.

The Dell, a steep-sided natural valley through which the River Hiraethlyn flows, is informally planted with a vast collection of shrubs and trees and in the summer the banks of the river are blue with hydrangeas which thrive in the damp, acid conditions. The choice conifers tower above the closely mown lawns.

As autumn approaches the garden takes on a different hue and this is a good time to study the varied foliage and barks of the maples, birches, sorbus and other shrubs which give a brilliant but restful display of autumn colour. Many coloured fruiting trees add to the autumn scene and, together with the foliage plants, make mid and late October a glorious end to the season.

Each autumn and winter new areas are developed and others improved: it is essential to have a continuous supply of plants so that the valuable collection is maintained. We are in the enviable position of having a large, modern propagation unit in which we can produce all our own plants for addition to the garden at a later date.

It is important that I think of t
future and it is a priority when planti
large specimen trees to place them
the correct position so that they do n
block vistas which may be created in t
future. It is often necessary to che
this from several angles; even a few fe
can make all the difference in twen
years time.

The garden's natural beauty mu
not be spoilt, but enhanced by skilf
colour-blending. Pastel colours con
bine easily but some of the reds ar
blues are difficult to place in certa
surroundings. Contrasts of foliage, sha
and colour are necessary in every gard
and, with careful selection, plantin
of outstanding effect can be achieve

Methods of cultivation, weed ar
pest control are changing but it is ofte
the traditional methods which prov
best; I am always looking to the futur
eager to try methods which will assi
me to maintain Bodnant in the be
condition.

Every garden must progress and it
not enough just to maintain a standar
we keep the best of the old but replac
the inferior and search for newe
superior forms. It is very hard work b
extremely interesting and rewarding;
look forward to the future of Bodnar
with every confidence and trust that
may play my part in maintaining it
high reputation for many years to come

3. Evening on Bodnant's top Rose Terrace,
looking beyond the Lily Terrace to the River
Conwy and part of the Snowdonia range. The
roses include 'Alexander', 'Rose Gaujard',
'Alec's Red', 'Glenfiddich', 'Ann Aberconway'
and 'Evelyn Fison'.   4. Two Atlas cedars
(*Cedrus atlantica glauca*) dominate the Lily
Terrace, with an evergreen oak behind. The
water lilies are selected hybrids, ranging in
colour from pink to red or white.   5. One of the
'secret' areas is this walk in the North Garden, a
profusion of selected deciduous azaleas, with the
plum-coloured Bodnant hybrid *Rhododendron*
'Youthful Sin' top left.   6. The Bodnant lewisia
(*Lewisia howellii* hybrids) grow in the Canal
Terrace drystone wall.   7. Late October in
Chapel Park, with Furnace Bank behind. Beyond
the red-berried *Sorbus scalaris* and the yellow
leaves of *Acer rubrum*, the orange foliage of
Sorbus commixta and the spectacular white-
berried *Sorbus cashmiriana* catch the autumn su

4.

7.

5.

6.

101

Cadogan Place Garden, London, SW1

KENWYN PEARSON

The Cadogan Place Garden has been in existence as a private fenced garden since the end of the eighteenth century. Some of the earliest formal plantings in the garden were made in the reign of Charles II, when mulberries were planted to help set up the silkworm industry. Unfortunately the wrong mulberry was planted, and the silkworm did not feed off the plants, but some of the trees still remain in the garden.

At the end of the eighteenth century Cadogan Place was designed as the London Botanic Garden, with a library, hothouse, greenhouse and conservatory and students of horticulture were trained here. From May to September on two evenings a week music was played in the garden for the benefit of subscribers. Subscribers paid one guinea per annum for the use of the garden and for two guineas they were permitted to bring in visitors as well. Strangers were allowed access to the garden for 2s. 6d. In 1820 the layout of the garden was changed and became more like it is today. Over the years little had altered in design or shape, but events were soon to change this.

The gardens are one of the few non-profit-making parts of the Estate. They are an amenity for the benefit of the residents, who subscribe to assist in their upkeep. Cadogan Place Garden is run by a management committee comprising residents, Estate officials and myself. The overall planning and policy is subject to committee approval. The gardens are very much appreciated by the residents and very well used, particularly in the summer, but like all green spaces in London, the garden has its regulars who take an active interest in the activities of the garden.

There have been few changes to the overall design of the garden, but in the last few years the emphasis has been towards more colour and variation, and labour-saving plantings. The first areas I developed were the entrances to the garden. Some of the shrubberies have now been replanted following the elm-felling programme, but some still need much work doing. I have a fairly free hand in deciding plants and plantings within the garden, and there are plenty of places to allow the more interesting and unusual plants to develop.

When I came to the Estate in January 1978, Cadogan Place Garden was undergoing a major change. Dutch elm disease had struck the garden and 135 trees had to be treated or felled. It took two years for complete removal, but the gap remaining in the eight acres of garden was immense. From the word go I could see great potential in the re-creation and development of a garden that had remained totally unchanged since the Second World War, with many of the old plantings now exhausted and many areas in desperate need of revitalization, to introduce colour and variation into the garden to create interest over the twelve months of the year. Hydrangeas and aucubas are fine and tolerate the London climate and soil, but since the Clean Air Acts and the reduction in pollution, and with London's unique micro-climate, it was obvious to me that a wider range of species could be grown in the 1980s. For the first twelve months I concentrated on cultivation, weed control and clearing the worst areas of the garden to remove rubbish tips, bonfire sites an ageing lilacs and philadelphus.

One of the first jobs was the replant ing of trees. After much discussion persuaded the Estate to embark on two- to three-year planting programm to introduce many tree species to th garden. For immediate effect four semi mature trees were planted. I was deter mined to introduce variety so that i the event of another attack like th elm disease, some of the trees woul be spared. It seemed desirable to intro duce more flowering species and als some coniferous subjects. Catalpa an paulownia thrive in London and, apar from a little protection in the first yea survive well from then on. Many di ferent acers now grow in the garden an trees like euodia and metasequoia als create interest. The soils are very fre draining and of a good depth, and th roots get a good run with few restric tions. It is now my policy to do som tree planting every year to ensur continuity. I fear the day when many the old London planes will have to b felled and there will be little to tak their place for many years, because o lack of foresight.

A large compost heap in the centre the garden was sifted and, after th removal of cans, bottles and othe household waste, the well-rotted ma terial was used to introduce some vari ation in level to what was largely a fla landscape. Within twelve months thi was to become a peat garden, support ing ericas, primulas and cyclamen. Th addition of *Cornus alba*, *C. stolonifer Viburnum fragrans* and *Clerodendro bungei* helped to create some effect fo winter. From under the brambles an ebris a very fine upright specimen of *Ginkgo biloba* emerged, now growing well and making a good shape. *Melianthus major, Decaisnea fargesii*, camellias and tree peonies make an attractive and workable group behind the peat bed, and *Ulex europaeus* and berberis are used to prevent too much traffic through the beds. Two large areas of the garden have been grassed over and naturalized with bulbs for spring display.

In the same area of the garden, climbing roses were planted to brighten the walls of the summer-houses. In another area close by, a holly hedge about five foot across was reduced to the bare stems and over the years will slowly grow back into a decent hedge. There is a large tennis court in the garden and the surrounding fence makes a good support for plants such as campsis, jasminum, tropaeolum and *Cobaea scandens*.

Hostas do very well in most parts of the garden, but I find meconopsis difficult to establish. *Plumbago capensis* overwinters in the sheltered spots as does oleander and the lovely *Rubus lineatus*.

All areas are pruned and cleaned in the winter, lightly forked over and mulched with leafmould and manure and fertilizer. Top dressings of peat are used in the peaty areas.

Bedding of sorts was arranged in three large beds in the garden. This was labour intensive and was proving very expensive; thousands of tulips were used. Slowly, over three years, I phased out two thirds of the bedding, replacing the tulips with rhododendrons and azaleas, and planting arbutus and hamamelis as a backing to give a good display, scent and the added bonus of autumn colour. The second bed I have turned into a mixed herbaceous and shrub border for all-year-round effect. Here iris flowers early in the year, leading on to mentha, nepeta, cistus, ceanothus, santolina, bearded iris, pentstemons, buddleias and others.

One large area of the garden, covered in elm, brambles, scrub and willowherb,

1. Ken Pearson on the Water Garden bridge; *Rheum palmatum* is in the foreground.

has now been cleared and, after being thoroughly dug and left bare for twelve months, is now the winter garden. Salix in variety provide winter stem effect, underplanted with cyclamens, aconites, snowdrops and narcissus.

Hellebores, with stransvaesia, kerria and photinia, give some interest in summer. A *Davidia involucrata* is now starting to make a fine specimen in this part of the garden.

When I plant new areas I always do so with the effect five years ahead in mind. This allows the plants to develop to a good size without competition and without any need for drastic thinning. I believe in good preparation for planting, particularly for trees. Where possible all my tree sites are dug in the summer preceding planting and left

open. This allows air and moisture to penetrate the site. I also like to plant before Christmas where possible so that the roots of the new trees can develop ready to draw the moisture up the tree at bud burst. I can honestly say I have few failures and the trees grow well.

The soil in the garden needed humus adding in copious amounts. The enormous number of trees in the garden has over the years sapped the energy from the soil. Organic matter has now been added and heavy mulching takes place each winter, particularly in newly planted areas. The winter of 1981–2 created many problems, with serious losses of some species. At the same time it opened up new vistas, with the possibility of further creation and the introduction of an even wider range of

plants. Hebes were lost by the dozen and had to be grubbed out. In 1982 fireblight became evident so some rosaceous species were also being hit.

A complete clearance of the beds and subsequent digging was carried out, and now a mixture of plants grows, with herbaceous material like symphytum as ground cover to smother weeds and create all-year-round interest. *Acacia dealbata*, *Jasminum wallichianum* and *Rosa rugosa* are creating pleasing effects. One of the great delights is the introduction of crocus flowering on the banks in the grassland areas. Naturalized in grass, and among trees and conifers, this is breathtaking, though there are the obvious difficulties in that the grass cannot be cut for at least eight weeks after the flowering of the bulbs.

The work never ceases to provide incentive and inspiration. There are so many hidden corners and parts to be developed, and numerous ideas to be

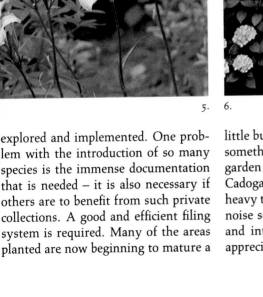

4.

5.   6.

explored and implemented. One problem with the introduction of so many species is the immense documentation that is needed – it is also necessary if others are to benefit from such private collections. A good and efficient filing system is required. Many of the areas planted are now beginning to mature a little but nature takes its time. There is something especially good about a large garden in London. When working in Cadogan Place it is easy to forget the heavy traffic of Sloane Street – even the noise seems to be lessened. The varied and interesting collection of plants is appreciated and visited by many people.

2. Spring in the Memorial Garden on the south lawn brings this showy display of *Prunus* 'Kanzan' with double purple-pink flowers.
3. Crocuses have been mass-planted in the North Garden for early visual effect, for the benefit of passers-by as well as the Cadogan Place residents.   4. The Rhododendron Walk provides colour for six weeks each year.
5. *Hemerocallis fulva* 'Bonanza'.   6. These hydrangeas are Hortensia hybrids, which grow well in London's poor soil.

Hall Place, Leigh, Tonbridge, Kent

PETER BEAGLEY

If ever there were a good example of the old saying about making a virtue out of necessity, I reckon that our gardens are it, in particular the Inner Garden at Hall Place.

Twenty-two years ago, I moved into the Victorian Gothick gardener's house here in the hop- and fruit-growing area of the Weald of Kent to become head gardener to the late Lord Hollenden. Hall Place, a vast mansion built in 1872, suffered a destructive fire in 1940 which left the east end, including the library, completely gutted. Although kept in repair, very little was done with this part until 1973 when the present Lord Hollenden took up residence and decided to make a garden there.

Our own garden has always been a joint effort, but my wife Audrey gives to it, I must admit, more thought than I do; my thoughts are never far away from the big garden.

In recent years, with a total staff of three in twenty acres of garden, pure maintenance work has taken up most of our time, leaving little time for alterations and new features. Lord Hollenden's Inner Garden project, therefore, afforded a welcome break from routine when, out of the ruins of the east end of Hall Place, we made a garden which is completely different from the more traditional areas.

Now, especially on an early spring morning, when the pink *Clematis montana* 'Elizabeth' flows over the far wall, the Inner Garden takes on a dream-like quality. This is particularly so when seen from the garden door of the house with the Dutch Garden and the Deer Park beyond.

Its planning evolved from discussions with Lord and Lady Hollenden, the agent and myself and, although it was originally planned to demolish the walls down to a uniform four feet, I suggested that most of the outer wall should be twelve feet, the height of the windows, thus giving height where plants could climb and hang.

Before demolition, we had to move precious shrubs temporarily from around the outer walls. However, a large *Hydrangea petiolaris* was left and protected against falling masonry while a very large specimen of *Magnolia grandiflora* was eased off the wall on to a frame constructed of scaffold boards where it stayed to the end of the job.

I well remember the morning in July 1975 when the demolition team arrived with a mobile crane, its seventy-foot jib just big enough to reach the finials and the chimney pots. It was a dramatic moment when the walls began to come down amid the dust and rubble.

The garden plan had been left to me and, when the old garden door surround was moved and built into the new outside wall of the house, we were able to take the stone slab step for our garden level to work from. At the far end we built two raised beds, two foot high.

1. Peter Beagley in the Dutch Garden.

2. The star of this view of the Inner Garden from the garden door is the hybrid musk rose 'Felicia'.

In May 1976, all of the original border plants outside the walls were returned to their homes and the *Magnolia grandiflora* was gently rested on two big old beams, supported by brick pillars specially built, as it stood well over the new wall height.

This intimate garden, although seen as an abundant whole where it is possible to indulge an interest in unusual plants as well as the soft colours of old favourites, was effectively divided into four areas, each bounded by crossing fine-gravel paths. Plants now overflow the paths nearer the house. Farther away, in the sitting area and, on the right, in an area of large pebbles with a York stepping-stone path leading to a vista over the lawns, the hard surfaces provide a foil for plants, like the white *Clematis montana* 'Alba', which hang from horizontal beams and others which tumble from the raised beds. Here also climbs the white *Clematis*

armandii, whose saucer-shaped flowers are borne in April; Lady Hollenden asked me to take cuttings from her favourite plant of it in London to bring to their new home, as she is fond of clematises in general.

In the sitting area we planted a golden philadelphus, *Euonymus radicans* 'Variegata', *Cotoneaster horizontalis*, *Euphorbia polychroma* and *Ceratostigma plumbaginoides*, as well as *Cytisus × kewensis* (profuse in May), *Dorycnium hirsutum* and *Sedum* 'Autumn Joy'. The purple *Clematis* 'H. E. Young' climbs up the wall and around the Victorian fireplace, which is sometimes used for barbecues. In the corner of this warmest area of the garden grow *Fremontia californica*, yellow flowered, and *Campsis radicans* 'Madame Galen', the trumpet creeper.

Nearer the house side is a goldfish pond surrounded by crazy paving; this is overlooked by the stone-pillared bay

window, preserved from demolition and now covered with wistaria, which goes up and over to join the *Magnolia grandiflora*. Also competing for a place is *Clematis rehderiana*, covered with little yellow, bell-shaped flowers; *Rosa* 'Dr W. van Fleet' grows around the buttress from the outside. In each of three corners of this area is a bed containing *Chamaecyparis lawsoniana* 'Fletcheri', now about seven feet high, underplanted with plants like *Alyssum* 'Gold Dust', *Erysimum* 'Bowles Mauve', *Cotoneaster congestus* and a collection of heathers. In one bed an *Acer japonica* gives the autumn colour for which acers are so prized. We built a rockery in the fourth corner and this is covered with *Artostaphylos Vya-Ursi*, *Chamaebuyus atro-purpurea* and *Dryas octopetala*, which allow spring bulbs to come through to give a little colour.

On the other side of the centre path, the left-hand area, is one big open soil bed where the soil was laid about five feet deep: it then settled down to about two feet in depth. In fact, all of the plants here are grown in no more than that depth of soil over the rubble created during demolition. However, this bed has such a collection of flourishing plants that, already, some have been removed.

In the far corner, a lovely drift of *Romneya trichocalyx* has rather taken over, with *Actinidia kolomikta* growing along the wall. Giving height already, standing at fourteen feet, is a specimen of *Chamaecyparis lawsoniana* 'Columnaris' with, growing beneath it, *Iris* 'Esther Faye' and *I.* 'Emmerdale' and a couple of interesting old hybrid perpetual roses, 'Baron Giraud-de-Lain' and the charming 'Roger Lamberlin'.

The old front door, still complete with its porch and tower, is now already covered with ivy and *Polygonum baldschuanicum* (the Russian vine) with the rambling rose Albéric Barbier joining the rush to the top.

There are 250 or so plants in the Inner Garden, many of them propagated from others in the gardens; most of them have flourished but small changes always need to be made, as in any garden.

At Gardener's House little was done for the first few years except the annual cutting of the hedges. Then, one day, much to my dismay, the big silver birch tree fell down; whether this was due to the building of new houses opposite, dislike of me or just old age I shall always wonder. It meant that, of necessity, I now had to make a garden.

It began with the planting of *Betula pendula* 'Dalecarlica', a tall, graceful birch with little spread, enabling planting almost beneath it with a group of conifers like chamaecyparis, thuja, *Juniperus* 'Skyrocket', *Picea pungens* and *P. glauca* and *Abies* 'Excelsa' underplanted with heathers.

Our house is in the corner of quite large area which, on our arrival, contained no flower borders, but had a lawn and a rather rough all-sorts hedge separating us from the stables, which, at that time, were used as a builder's yard.

Eventually, a privet hedge near the house was removed to give way to a new rose bed where we planted 'Peace' and 'Pink Favourite'. Between the kitchen door and the hedge we made a lawn surrounded by beds and stone sinks. These are Audrey's particular interest; the hanging baskets, with fuchsias and geraniums, which improve the look of the brickwork in this area, are largely due to her.

On the far side of the south lawn a truly mixed border, backed by the field beyond, runs the full length of the lawn; annuals, perennials, shrubs and

3. Over the end wall of the Inner Garden, with the Dutch Garden beyond, flows *Clematis montana* 'Elizabeth'.

4.

5.

6.

trees all flourish here with two *Thuja plicata*, twenty feet high. Here also a *Robinia pseudoacacia* 'Frisia' contrasts well with *Philadelphus coronarius* 'Aureus', *Spiraea* 'Gold Flame' and the brilliant *Rhododendron* 'Cynthia'. We are always experimenting and, this year, we have tried out the red, tall-growing *Meconopsis napaulensis* in association with other plants.

At right angles to the long border, a smaller one divides the garden from the stable area and, nearer the house, the sitting area is backed by a carefully clipped high yew hedge. A new addition to the lawn is a rather attractive fish pond, another of Audrey's particular interests; already she has planted all kinds of water plants, which are growing well.

However, when all is said, it is the plants that make a garden, not the features. I have a great respect for resilient, self-seeding plants and most enjoy the natural effect one can achieve by encouraging them to grow happily and informally in the company of each other.

4. Nicotiana and *Phlomis fruticosa* soften the stone at the entrance to the Inner Garden. Two tubs are planted with pelargoniums and trailing silver plants.   5. The Gardener's House lawn is surrounded by beds filled with colour: in the foreground is *Rhododendron* 'Cynthia'. 6. Wallflowers and species tulips flourish in formal tubs at Gardener's House and Audrey Beagley's sinks have *Juniperus communis* 'Compressa' sharing space with favourite miniature plants. In the border, saxifrages, dwarf narcissus and myosotis complete the spring scene.

Sandringham House, Norfolk

FRED WAITE

Sandringham has been a royal residence since 1862 and since that time each successive head gardener has made changes.

I have been fortunate in that most of the major changes have been made during the period in which I have been head gardener and some of my own ideas have been implemented.

Every year since 1967, an area of the grounds has been selected, with Her Majesty the Queen's approval, for re-planning and replanting.

Before the programme of replanting started, which was to be phased over many years, advice was sought from the late Sir Eric Savill, Keeper of the Savill Gardens, Windsor, and later from Mr Hope Findlay, also of the Savill Gardens, whose help and advice is still greatly appreciated.

Before planting, each area was cleared of most of the trees and shrubs, which consisted mainly of laurel (*Prunus laurocerasus*), *Aucuba japonica*, *Rhododendron ponticum* and berberis yew, at the same time retaining the screen around the perimeter of the grounds to ensure some privacy for the royal family. These had no doubt originally been planted as fillers but over the years had outgrown the choice plants. Every gardener, amateur or professional, falls into the trap of sometimes failing to cut back or grub out a strong happy plant in order to allow the choice slow growing plant to flourish.

At Sandringham, this no doubt happened over many years due to the shrinking labour force, particularly during the war years when there was little maintenance on shrub beds and the emphasis was on the production of food in the kitchen garden. The old kitchen gardens no longer exist as such and the area is used to produce soft fruit.

We have kept the better specimens of *Cercidiphyllum japonicum, Pinus maritima* (Corsican pine), *Davidia involucrata* (handkerchief tree), betula (birch), magnolia and *Aesculus indica*, and incorporated them in the new landscaping.

The original layout included very narrow paths, just wide enough for the owners and their friends to walk around, so one of the priorities was to make wider paths, taking into consideration the hundreds of thousands of visitors who come each year, from April to September.

The replanting was never dense, allowing the perennial weeds to be forked out by hand during the spring and summer. The following winter the whole area was mulched to a depth of four inches with leafmould from the nearby woods. This helped to reduce the germination of annual weeds and to retain moisture – very necessary despite an irrigation system which pumps water from the spring-fed Lower Lake, for Sandringham is in a low-rainfall area and has a dry soil. The correct choice of plants is essential, taking into account shade, moisture and soil conditions in any one area.

The earliest planting started by Norwich Gates in 1967 and consisted mainly of rhododendrons, azaleas, magnolias and hydrangeas. Before any planting could be undertaken around the lakes, large areas of dense-rooted bamboos had to be removed. These were obscuring an excellent vista into the dell, with a magnificent mature *Magnolia denudata* forming the focal point. Alongside the Upper Lake, a bold group of *Gunnera scabra*, its gigantic leaves six feet across and standing on a seven-foot stem, contrasts with the background of feathery bamboos.

Rising from the banks of the Upper Lake stands a bold carrstone rockery and boathouse. No alpines are grown on the rockery because of the large amount of hand-weeding that would be involved, so an interesting collection of dwarf conifers has been planted, making the area much easier to maintain.

Where the Upper Lake flows into the Lower Lake, a waterfall has been created, and the surrounding area has been planted with August- and September-

1. Fred Waite.

Sandringham House.

flowering heathers interspersed with dwarf conifers and ground-hugging junipers. Some of the heathers chosen are *Calluna vulgaris* 'My Dream', with brilliant double white flowers, 'County Wicklow', double pink, 'Darkness', crimson, and 'J. H. Hamilton', bright double pink; *Erica carnea* 'Fox Hollow', grown for its pink and red foliage; and *Erica cinerea* 'Velvet Night', with purple, almost black flowers and 'St Kelverne', bright rose.

Junipers incorporated are *J. horizontalis* 'Hughes', 'Blue Moon', 'Emerald Spreader', 'Glauca' and 'Grey Pearl', *J. media* 'Mint Julep' and 'Old Gold', *J. sabina* 'Buffalo' and 'Rockery Gem', and *J. virginiana* 'Silver Spreader'.

In 1981, it was decided to replant a boggy area below Jubilee Lodge, which was a new and exciting venture. An open ditch was dug allowing bog and moisture-loving plants to be introduced, which greatly widened the range of varieties of plants grown in the grounds. Caltha, also known as marsh marigold or kingcups, are grown in the ditch. This I find one of the delights of

spring; the new growth is unfortunately a favourite diet of the water vole. Also grown here are *Iris laevigata*, *Pontederia cordata* and *Scirpus zebrinus*, a striking species of variegated rush with alternating bands of green and yellow down the stem, *Lysichitum americanum*, a striking bog plant of the arum family, which has bright yellow flowers in April, and *L. camtschatcense*, which is of similar habit but has white flowers. Several varieties of dwarf pussy willow grow on the bank, namely *Salix hastata* with grey catkins and grey leaves, *S. helvetica*, with silver leaves and golden catkins, *Salix lanata*, with yellow catkins and silver leaves and *S. melanostachys*, which has almost black catkins opening to yellow before the leaves appear, together with *Agapanthus* 'Headbourne Hybrids', astilbe in a wide variety of colours ranging from white to red, my favourite being *A. chinensis pumila*, with mat-forming foliage and delicate pink spikes. The ditch runs into a stream, the layout of which has been improved by the building of small waterfalls and widening in places to

form almost still pools. Now a wide range of plants may be grown. Use has been made of the coloured-stemmed *Cornus stolonifera* 'Flaviramea' (yellow stems) and *Cornus alba* 'Westonbirt' (red stems), excellent plants for colour and reflection in the winter sunlight. There are now many varieties of primula flourishing here, although this is a plant that we have had difficulty growing in the drier areas of the grounds.

Varieties of rodgersia have been planted in the ditch and stream area. This is a useful, tolerant plant with handsome chestnut-like foliage. It will withstand wind and sun, but, like filipendula, it needs plenty of moisture. The choicest rodgersia, I think, is *R. ulmaris* 'Aurea', which forms golden mounds of foliage. The flowers are less attractive and the two-foot stem is best removed to promote new foliage.

Along the edges of the paths ranunculus (the buttercup family) have been planted, the most unusual being *R. aconitifolius plenus* with its double white button flowers from May to July;

3. A favourite formal area of Sandringham at the north end of the house, planted with a collection of annuals and perennials including peonies, sweet peas, catmint, lychnis and thalictrum.

also ajuga with its carpet-like foliage of red, purple, bronze, gold and green. Hemerocallis (the day lily) are established around the lake and new varieties have been planted alongside the ditch and stream. These new varieties have the widest range of colours. I find this a most valuable and tolerant plant.

I have tried to create a garden which has some colour and interest at all times of the year and to avoid a specialist garden which is magnificent for a short period but may have little to offer for the rest of the year. This has its difficulties, but I have found the hardy fuchsia very useful for providing colour when most of the shrubs are past their best. They are in flower from July until the first frost and have proved to be much hardier than one might think. All the varieties grown at Sandringham, of which there are over seventy, have withstood twenty-five degrees of frost without any losses. This is partly due to the free-draining soil, as fuchsias do not like waterlogged conditions during a severe winter.

Among the varieties grown are one of the oldest, *Fuchsia pumila*, introduced as far back as 1821, and a much more recent introduction called 'Prosperity', which is one of my favourites. It has very large double flowers of crimson and rose. My love of fuchsias may have stemmed from the early part of my gardening career when I was with Mr Percy Thrower at Shrewsbury, where many varieties are grown. It is nice to see some of the older varieties such as 'Brutus', 'Constance', 'Abbé Farges', 'Brilliant', 'Achievement' and 'Riccartonii' being grown as hardy plants. For many years they were considered too tender and were grown mainly as pot plants.

Hostas have been planted under various conditions in the gardens and have adapted themselves well. They are most vigorous where there is ample moisture and shade, especially the more variegated varieties such as *H. fortunei* 'Aurea' which is not happy in direct sunlight. Lavender, on the other hand, is happiest in the full sun; many different lavenders are grown, ranging in colour from white and pink through all the different shades of blue to the deepest purple.

Another sun-loving plant is *Oenothera missouriensis*. This is an easy plant to raise from seed. It spreads quickly and produces pale lemon cup-shaped flowers. A south-facing border or bank site is ideal. Dry shade is every one's biggest problem and in these areas we grow varieties of ivy, vinca, cotoneaster and *Ruscus aculeatus* (butcher's broom), the latter being very popular for flower arranging, particularly at Christmas.

The development of a garden this size depends on having a willing band of workers who work as a team and take a pride in the job. Throughout my career at Sandringham I have been fortunate in having such men on my staff. However, my task would have been impossible but for the interest and encouragement given by Her Majesty and Mr Julian Loyd, the land agent at Sandringham.

5.

6.

. This delightful vista of a wide variety of hydrangeas has, in the foreground, the pyramidal white anicles of *H. paniculata* 'Grandiflora'.   5. Fred Waite has led the development of this stream garden y the Jubilee Gates, here showing hostas, hemerocallis and astilbes in July.   6. There are, in this eature bed of lavender, seven different varieties and colours.   7. October shows this recent planting f heathers and dwarf conifers at their best.

7.

Orchard House, 266 Cowley Road, Uxbridge, Middlesex

DON DRAKE

I could be regarded as a one-man garden designer and construction unit, but with my appreciation and love of plants, I consider myself to be a very rare form of jobbing gardener. I am fortunate enough to have clients over a thirty-mile radius, not only in London but also in Berkshire and Buckinghamshire.

A new client of mine said to me recently, 'I expect I'm one of the *nouveau riche* but, as I'm rather proud of my new garden, will you please make sure that, as you plan it, visitors can see into every corner at one go?' He needs

educating! I prefer to give to even the smallest garden secret areas.

More often than not clients do need converting, not only about the layout of their gardens but also to more interesting plants. I usually get rid of bedding plants, although I will tolerate geraniums in pots. Many people, however well heeled, don't know what I am talking about at first, being frightened by plant names, and so, quite often, I take them to the RHS Gardens at Wisley or to my own garden to see the plants.

Some of my clients share my taste

and enthusiasm for plants like old and species roses and, by encouraging them I am able to enjoy new plants in their gardens for which I no longer have room at home, my garden being so full.

I have had the ground-floor flat at Orchard House since 1971; the house set in a three-quarter-acre plot on busy main road, is L-shaped, facing south and east, with a wing protecting the part of my garden which is nearest the house. The owner, John Nicholls lives in the upper flat and, since he has been happily planting shrubs, trees and

1. Don Drake.

. The cool chaos of Don Drake's 'other garden'.

erbaceous plants here since 1928, I ave learned a great deal from him.

When I moved in, the 21 × 40 foot arden nearest the house consisted of a cruffy lawn bounded by a wattle fence n the north, with skimmias and camel- as appearing over it, an ivy-covered tump with some mixed shrubs on the ast and a free standing wistaria, roses nd a *Magnolia stellata* backing the bed n the south.

It had distinct possibilities; I added brick paving to an existing stone-paved area outside my French windows, a brick panel round a very large oblong stone sink in the south border (making a good focal point from the entrance) and a D-shaped brick panel at the far end beyond the lawn, now carefully maintained. In this area, a low retaining wall was built for a raised bed to form a focal point from the house.

The visitor approaches my garden through a simple archway formed of black cast-iron pipes, on which is trained a well-established claret vine (*Vitis vinifera purpurea*). This is at its best in autumn, when it is bearing grapes, particularly when the sun shines through the richly dark leaves.

Immediately inside are the tall spikes of *Phormium tenax*, the *rugosa* rose 'Blanc Double de Coubert' and a specimen of *Rosa rubrifolia*, interplanted with the variegated *Hebe* 'Silver Wraith' and various treasures.

Having a fondness for large-growing subjects with special foliage interest, I planted *Viburnum rhytidophyllum*, the elegant and slender *Phylostachis aurea* and *Amelanchier laevis*, a tree which gives a full twelve months of interest in flower, berry, leaves and twiggy winter tracery.

I have developed a passion for two or three groups of plants but for none more than euphorbias and in this part of my garden I planted both *E. wulfenii* (which bushes up to four feet with thick columns of yellow-green flower bracts, maturing in May to July) and *E. palustris* (smaller but with heads, 4–6 inches wide, of sulphur-yellow bracts). Here also are madonna lilies, gold-margined hostas, a fine white tree peony ('Haku-o-Jishi') and many ferns, including the hart's tongue, shield, shuttlecock and bird's foot.

The paved terrace is enlivened by nine square earthenware pans, each containing a different sempervivum, fringed in between by the golden *Helexine aurea* which forms a pleasant contrast to the austere shapes of the sempervivums. Above spreads the beautiful golden-leaved weigela.

The house wall is clad with two roses ('Gloire de Dijon' and 'Mermaid'), *Clematis armandii* 'Snowdrift', *Trachelospermum japonicum* and the winter-flowering *Jasminum nudiflorum*.

Farther down the garden, beyond John Nicholls's collection of hybrid Bourbon roses, is a rather less formal area which he made available to me. While it is much softer, it is also more wild, full of plants set in beds whose dividing paths wind around two well-

4.

3.

3. Don Drake made and maintains this garden
for a client in Gerrards Cross. Its intimacy is
underlined by the offsetting of various textures
of plants with each other in beds set in an
expanse of lawn. Plants include santolina, *Yucca
filamentosa*, *Sedum maximum* 'Atropurpureum';
schizostylis, heathers, *Potentilla* 'Elizabeth' and
rosemary.   4. His own small alpine beds
abound with numerous helianthemums.
Euphorbia wulfenii, spiraea and the long grass
Helictotrichon sempervirens are among the
plants surrounding the beds.   5. In Don Drake's
other garden at Orchard House, the view from
under the apple tree includes sisyrinchiums,
penstemons and the extremely vigorous
climbing rose 'Wedding Day'.   6. His own
garden near the house with ordered plantings of
Hosta 'Aureo-variegata', *Salvia superba*,
Geranium psilostemon, *Zantedeschia aethiopica*
'Crowborough' and *Hosta sieboldiana* 'Elegans'.

116

grown apple trees ('James Grieve' and 'Blenheim Orange'). It is, in effect, the dumping ground for many of the plants which, compulsively, I have bought at garden openings, plant sales and nurseries. But I love it.

About 20 × 80 feet, it is bounded by a wire fence on which John has trained blackberries; on the other side is a clipped thorn hedge where I have tried my hand at topiary. Each apple tree is set in a small round bed, one filled with *Euphorbia robbiae*, which thrives in the shade, with dark green, leathery leaves, and the other with the evergreen fern *Polystichum setiferum*.

The scalloped borders on either side contain a harmonious jungle of shrubs and plants, including a thicket of bamboos (another passion), among them *Arundinaria nitida*, with purple stems and bright green, bristly margined leaves, and *Sasa veitchii*. Among the shrubs are the beautiful variegated *Cornus alternifolia* with horizontally spreading, light-leaved branches, *Rosa primula* (a yellow species rose) and the arching, light yellow 'Frühlingsgold', an aralia and hebes. I lost an imposing bush of *Hebe cupressoides* after a heavy snowfall and a 'Golden Wings' rose by honey fungus, which is endemic around here, but I managed to save the *primula* rose by an injection of Amillatox.

The underplanting includes a large mature clump of *Helleborus orientalis*, in a fine, mulberry-red form, and *H. corsicus*. The former flowers wonderfully in February, *H. corsicus* flowers in March with cup-shaped, yellow-green flowers.

I may have gone slightly over the top with my euphorbias: *E. wulfenii, E. coraloides, E. amygdaloides purpurea, E. dulcis, E. griffithii* and *E. sikkimensis* are all here. A grey patch includes artemisia, lavender, cotton lavender and senecio; there is a group of *Thalictrum dipterocarpum*, 4–5 feet tall, with loose sprays of minute mauve flowers; and variegated forms of *Anchusa myosotidiflora, Sisyrinchium striatum, Yucca filamentosa* and *Crambe cordifolia* with a *Clematis* 'Niobe' near by to clamber over it.

Despite the pressure of the roots and shade cast by the apple trees, all the plants and shrubs are outgrowing their positions and the garden is in danger of becoming uncontrolled, partly because I loathe fiddling around with secateurs just to snip bits off here and there.

At the entrance to this area, I have created an open square of low brick terraces, filled with an open, gravelly mixture for nearly fifty alpines and nine small shrubs, the bricks taking the place of natural rock.

I cannot resist the temptation to buy plants; I buy them and am immediately faced with the problem of finding a suitable home but sometimes they replace plants which have become decrepit or have succumbed to a difficult winter.

In my clients' gardens it's a different matter; there the planting must be more disciplined and I have to control it. Either way, it's a great occupation.

117

Girton College, Cambridge

STEPHEN W. BEASLEY

My interest in conservation and the natural landscape was encouraged while I was working in local government in the West Midlands by my bosses, Ken Williams and Iain Hodson, and the main reason for accepting the post at Girton in 1980 was that there appeared to be an excellent opportunity here for continuing this interest.

Girton College was founded in 1869 as the first college for women in this country and it has long been surrounded by gardens which are the least formal and the most unpredictable of all Cambridge college gardens.

The college was built a mile and a half away from the city to ensure that the ladies were not distracted from their studies by the city's social life. The gardens therefore played an important recreational role in the lives of the undergraduates and do to this day, with summer picnics in the honeysuckle walk and barbecue parties in the Old Orchard.

Designed by the Waterhouses, father and son, from 1872 until 1932, Girton underwent five major alterations and additions and the gardens grew and changed with these random developments, which seem to have added further to their charm.

Gertrude Jekyll was originally commissioned to design planting schemes for the cloister courtyard but these were never carried out. I wonder if, even in 1910, the cost and labour involved in the management of such features were realized, though I am told that there were upwards of fifteen gardeners (we have five). Encompassed within its fifty-five acres are formal rose gardens, enclosed courtyards, a large pond, annual bedding displays, a nursery, the honeysuckle walk and two orchards, one of which is the main subject of this chapter. All are enclosed by a delightful woodland walk of over a mile around the college.

Undergraduates are encouraged to use the garden and are even allowed to walk on the grass! This does cause problems in maintaining an acceptable standard, but at least the gardens are used and appreciated by members of the college.

On my arrival here, working discussions with the Garden Committee centred around the creation of a wild garden within the grounds. We looked at the Old Orchard which was already established as a favourite recreational spot and the committee particularly wanted to retain it rather than turn it to commercial advantage. At least eighty years old, being first mentioned in the 1904 college records, the Old Orchard is unique in that it contains some sixty cultivars of apple, very few of which are now grown commercially, a few plums and pears and a holly tree which never fails to provide berries for Christmas. Worthy of conservation in its own right, the orchard became the ideal setting for the creation of the wild flower meadow.

My first task, for once, was to let the grass grow under my feet for a season. This enabled me to identify any areas of existing flora and wet/dry areas, take pH tests and, while the grass was growing, identify all the apple cultivars. Then, during the winter, around a log fire, fittingly made from an ancient 'Blenheim Orange' which blew down in a storm, the information was collated.

A development and management plan was drawn up, incorporating the need for spraying and feeding the fruit trees (anathema in itself to the welfare of wild flowers) and for access to most of the trees for fruit picking, while not restricting the orchard's recreational use.

The plan is to achieve a wild flower meadow to cover over half of the orchard area; this will be in several drifts, that is areas joined together by meandering, close-mown paths. Here and there the paths will widen out to form secret enclosures, some within the wild flower drifts and some amongst tall grasses where one can sit under an apple tree and study, sunbathe, picnic or just watch the butterflies.

The choice of flowers is divided into two distinct groups: the first is a general mixture suitable for our soil conditions and the second is a more specialized group containing the rarer species with emphasis on the Cambridgeshire flora, providing a reservoir for their survival.

In the autumn of 1981 I began to sow seeds collected from a few cowslips (*Primula veris*) which were already growing in the orchard. The seeds were mixed with a little damp, fine sand, which is always a good way of sowing very small seed. As a result, we now have a small but thriving community of cowslips, although some appear to have been tempted by the charms of their garden relatives and have cross-pollinated with polyanthus.

In another area of the orchard I have been able to introduce a further group of cowslips by courtesy of Erica Swale, who gave me some grown from plants taken from the same orchard many

1. Stephen Beasley.

rye grass, called 'Tama', is now recommended, but I have no experience of it yet. I should mention that, if the soil is very fertile, especially clay, it is better not to use a nurse grass as it is much too vigorous; simply sow the flower seeds alone.

I am only just beginning the work required after the establishment of our small areas but this is aimed at attempting to maintain a balance between species. Depending on what wild flowers are growing, one cut or, at the most, two cuts a season is all that is needed once the meadow is established. The first cut is done in late July or early August when most of the flowers have seeded and then, possibly, in early November, to control the species which are vigorous over the winter period. When we have larger areas established the plan is to split each drift into two areas, cutting each part later in alternate years to give any later-flowering species a chance to seed; it all helps to maintain and ensure the balance and diversity of the species.

Remember that seeds should not be collected from the wild, as many species are protected. The choice of which species to grow is vast and depends on so many things, not least what you want to achieve. Most good seed houses now offer ready-mixed collections for different uses and soil conditions, and individual species can be bought as required. For my own part, I bought a standard mix plus one or two additions which I particularly wanted to introduce; the mix includes agrimony, cornflower, meadow cranesbill and ragged robin.

Wild flowers are encouraged in other areas of the gardens, especially in the woodlands where, beneath the shelter of the trees, they thrive undisturbed. Our first sign of spring is the winter aconite (*Eranthis hyemalis*) underneath the horse chestnuts lining the main entrance to the college. They start to flower in early January, completely carpeting the ground by mid-February, and are followed by snowdrops and daffodils, mainly naturalized forms which

years ago, a real example of practical conservation in action. At the same time, I have been careful not to mow out little groups of poppies, celandines and bluebells which, although a bit of a mixed bag, are just as welcome in our meadow. Our daffodil glade, tucked away in a corner of the orchard, is a mass of bloom in the spring, all grown from bulbs used in glasshouse forcing and then naturalized outside.

There are several ways of establishing a wild flower meadow; I use the most common whereby the wild flowers are sown with a 'nurse crop' of grass seed which, because it becomes established much more quickly than the flowers, provides a protective canopy over the wild flowers, helps prevent undesirable seed invasion and, in an exposed site, helps reduce soil erosion. It is vital that, once the nurse grass's job is done, it is removed, so I use an annual rye grass which must be cut before it seeds – one called 'Westerwolds' works very well. An improved cultivar of this flower in the more open area. A recent felling of a large area of dead trees has resulted in a definite increase in the number of blooms.

From late April to June, the woodlands are especially delightful; honesty (*Lunaria annua*) and bluebells (*Endymion non scriptus*) flower in small groups wherever they please and, a little later, cow parsley (*Anthriscus sylvestris*), long established at Girton, is joined by great leopard's bane (*Doronicum pardalianches*). This is an attractive association which I first saw as a student near Reading and now encourage here.

That spectacular garden escape the giant hogweed (*Heracleum mantegazzianum*) has recently arrived at Girton and is so invasive it needs careful watching; it is, of course, poisonous; if it is touched, it may cause the skin to blister in sunny weather.

The work of the National Council for the Conservation of Plants and Gardens is also concerned with work of a similar nature and this has led me to help form the Cambridgeshire group, for whom I am carrying out a survey of the private gardens within the county which are either noteworthy in themselves or are scheduled for redevelopment and contain plants worth preserving.

Anyone who plants and maintains a wild flower garden, no matter how small, is helping to redress a balance which has seen 95 per cent of our natural wild flower meadows disappear under the plough since the Second World War.

2.

2. Winter aconites (*Eranthis hyemalis*) brighten the main college entrance in mid-February.
3. An attractive association of cow parsley (*Anthriscus sylvestris*) and leopard's bane (*Doronicum pardalianches*) at the woodland edge. 4. Cowslips (*Primula veris*) have recently been established by Steve Beasley in the Old Orchard; cross-pollination with the garden polyanthus produces the colour changes.
5. *Heracleum mantegazzianum.* 6. This unusual collection of sixty-four varieties of prize-winning apple cultivars is also a much-used recreation area for Girton's students.

4.

5.

6.

Polesden Lacey, Dorking, Surrey

ROBERT HALL

The present house and thirty-acre garden at Polesden Lacey are beautifully set among the woods on the chalk of the North Downs and have associations with the eighteenth-century playwright Richard Brinsley Sheridan, who lived in an earlier house on the same site. The Long or Sheridan Walk was lengthened by him during his time here.

However the National Trust is maintaining the Edwardian atmosphere of the present house, which was adapted in 1906 by the last private owner, the Hon. Mrs Ronald Greville, from a Regency original. With a staff of four, I have the task of preserving this feeling in the gardens.

Apart from the long grassed Sheridan Walk, predominant features are the numerous stone ornaments, vistas, large trees and wide lawns. Polesden Lacey is not usually regarded as a 'plantsman's garden' but, on closer examination, garden enthusiasts find more of horticultural interest than they expect.

Mrs Greville created the Rose Garden by a remarkable transformation of the nineteenth-century walled kitchen garden. There are 2,400 bush roses in rectangular beds with shrub roses round the edge which are interplanted with delphiniums and hardy fuchsias and underplanted with various ground-cover plants to give a softening effect.

This continues with climbers on the inside walls; a particularly effective blend is that of Clematis 'Victoria' and C. 'Perle d'Azur' growing through the creamy-yellow rose 'Mermaid'.

Six years ago we reconstructed the extensive rose-covered pergola, using treated local pine in preference to larch which had previously been found unsatisfactory. The colour scheme is Edwardian, avoiding 'hot' colours and keeping as nearly as possible to white, pink, crimson and light yellow.

Because of the shallow, chalky soil the beds were excavated to a depth of eighteen inches and replaced with good-quality Cranleigh loam in 1938, but nothing lasts for ever and, when the budget allows, we replant one rose bed a year. During the advance preparation we treat each bed with Basamid soil sterilant; in fact, we are now extending the treatment to other suitable areas.

Gardeners often think that their particular problems are unique and I am not much different! My problems are the very dry nature of the North Downs chalk and its limitations. The rhododendron and associated 'American Garden' connoisseurs tend to look down their noses at the chalk gardener but it is surprising what can be grown here; the failure of some plants may be due as much to the lack of moisture as to the excessive lime.

The 150-yard herbaceous border has been a problem in this respect for some time; facing due south, it is backed by a high, heat-reflecting brick wall. Dry, hot weather dries it out badly and our watering system is inadequate. However, by the slow trial-and-error process of discarding some plants and

1. Polesden Lacey House from the South Terrace in autumn.

introducing others which may be more suitable, coupled with heavy mulching, we seem to be winning.

In order to maintain the Edwardian atmosphere, it is necessary to avoid the temptation to leave one's own trademark. There are, all the same, two east-facing, yew-backed borders with which I particularly identify. They happen to lead up to our own Victorian gabled house, which is quite picturesque, particularly in midsummer when the 'Maigold' rose, right next to our Ceanothus 'Edinburgh', climbs and arches out from the gable with its white-painted, finely carved bargeboards and finials.

However, several years ago these particular borders were due to be grassed over in the interests of economy, to leave a more orderly, symmetrical but considerably less interesting area. I prefer to retain as much horticultural interest as possible and, somehow, managed to negotiate a stay of execution. The borders have now been completely replanted and, being rather more moisture retentive than other parts of the garden, now support some of the plants that do not succeed in the drier long border. Some emphasis was put on plants which flower relatively early in the season to fill a gap and overlap with and follow on from the spring bulbs elsewhere.

This idea has been only partially adhered to, although a number of plants do begin flowering quite early on, in particular Euphorbia polychroma, Doronicum 'Miss Mason' and Lathyrus vernus. These are followed closely by the pale blue spikes of Veronica gentianoides and by Fritillaria pyrenaica, the latter being a real gem with its unusual bell-like flowers in shades of greenish and purplish brown externally with a contrasting greenish yellow when you look up inside the bells.

Peonies also do well just here, and in the two peony borders elsewhere in the gardens. P. 'Bowl of Beauty' is a truly magnificent sight for all too short a period during the latter part of June. Just one departure from the herbaceous

2. Robert Hall with Garden Cottage behind.

nature of the borders has become a tradition – a bay is now always reserved for an annual planting of mignonette, with its old-fashioned charm and unique scent.

Adjoining the southern side of my own garden, and enclosed on three sides by yew and box hedges, is the Winter Garden. This name is somewhat misleading because, although it does contain quite a few winter-flowering plants, it is at its most spectacular in early spring. Three large iron trees

(Parrotia persica) form the centrepiece and produce crimson tassel-like flowers during February. They have the additional value of autumn colour as the leaves turn to magnificent shades of crimson and gold at the end of the season. In early spring, however, they are carpeted beneath by a variety of bulbs, the earliest of these being snowdrops.

The first real splash of colour is provided by the winter aconites (Eranthis hyemalis), a welcome carpet of gold at

123

3.

a time that can appear bleak and uncompromising. The pale blue *Scilla tubergeniana* also puts in an early appearance. This is planted in a large group rather than a naturalized mass and has the curious habit of opening its topmost flowers almost at ground level as they push through the soil. The many other naturalized bulbs then follow on in profusion: crocuses, chionodoxas, *Iris reticulata*, *Scilla siberica*, *Cyclamen vernum* and muscari.

Among the earliest-flowering shrubs the sweet box (sarcococca), in several species, and *Mahonia japonica* are probably the most effective. While not exactly showy in flower, their sweet, penetrating fragrances intermingle and scent the air. This alone attracts people towards the Winter Garden to locate the source of the scent.

The Winter Garden is bounded on the north side by a yew hedge, behind which my own garden is still developing; one of the disadvantages to living on top of the job is that, like the cobbler's children's shoes, there is rarely time to do your own garden. So far, behind the house, I have made a Summer Garden out of the former garden rubbish tip, gradually planting little treasures tending towards the cool colours, particularly white. One particular success is the golden rain tree, *Koelreuteria paniculata*, which I raised from seed some years ago.

Outside our kitchen door is a small, cool, paved area for summer days: it is greatly enhanced by plants in containers around the edge; in season *Hydrangea* 'Libella', in an oak tub, is truly magnificent, bearing pure white lacecap flowers. Adding different textures, there is a small fan palm (*Trachycarpus fortunei*), a young 'White Marseilles' fig and various hostas. We also use one or other of the golden-variegated and the silver-variegated forms of *Aralia elata*; these are vastly underrated architectural plants of great value, but they are quite expensive and not always easy to find.

On the other side of the house, tucked away behind the yews, is my

3. Garden Cottage overlooks the Winter Garden and is seen in February through branches of *Parrotia persica*, over a carpet of winter aconites (*Eranthis hyemalis*) and snowdrops.

4. In June the south face of Garden Cottage, standing at the end of an overflowing herbaceous border, is wreathed in *Ceanothus* 'Edinburgh' and the yellow rose 'Maigold'.   5. The climbing rose 'Albertine', racing over the Rose Garden pergola, frames 'Cornelia' beyond. In the background are 'Yellow Pages' and 'Rose Gaujard'.   6. This glimpse of Polesden Lacey house from the Rose Garden includes 'Penelope' roses in the foreground and, behind, 'Frensham' and 'Escapade'.

4.

5.

6.

vegetable plot, where I attempt my own version of a three-year rotation. I have also started to play around with two short rows of grape vines trained on posts and wires, using the French 'Double Guyot' training system; I plan, eventually, to try another two rows on the 'Geneva Double Curtain' system. The varieties are mainly 'Muller-Thurgau', with two each of 'Chardonnay' and 'Wrotham Pinot' at one end.

This purely domestic enterprise is the logical conclusion to a number of visits to commercial vineyards in southern England when, on each occasion, the end product was sampled and my enthusiasm fired. I have no grand plans for developing a Polesden Lacey vineyard but this plot would appear to be well-suited, being on a gentle, south-facing slope, overlying chalk.

Pusey House Gardens, Faringdon, Oxfordshire

KEN COTTON

When I first came to Pusey House Gardens eleven years ago for interview, on a dull, wet day, I had been certain that I would not take the job. My first impression, in the rain, was only of a very large garden in which I saw little beauty through my rain-splashed spectacles.

However, Mr and Mrs Hornby persuaded me to come back with my family. We arrived on a beautiful June day to an entirely different garden; the sun was shining through the trees and making wonderful reflections on the clear water of the lake. The birds were singing and the shrub roses and herbaceous plants were beginning to burst into colour, showing the artistry and care that had been used in creating one of the best gardens in the country, a Garden of Eden in Oxfordshire.

1. Ken Cotton.

Pusey House Gardens were mostly created following the last war, although my employers bought the house in 1935. The lake, wonderfully planted by the Chinese bridge, is the great central feature now, although then it was found as a trickle of water in a large expanse of mud. Visitors reach it beyond a double herbaceous border planted in the colours of the rainbow, through the ornamental gates leading to a whole vista of lawns, woods and shrubberies.

Rose Cottage, the gardener's house, overlooks my favourite part of the gardens, Lady Emily's Garden – named after Lady Emily Herbert who married Philip Bouverie-Pusey in 1822, a founder of the Royal Agricultural Society. This walled garden, twenty yards square, is divided into four parts by two flagstone paths running through the garden like a cross. In the centre there is a sundial with two metal arches crossed over it, covered with climbing roses and clematis. Four inner beds are planted with the lovely H T rose 'Violinista Costa'. In the four outer beds are various plants such as penstemon, phlox, *Alstroemeria ligtu* hybrids, platycodon (the blue balloon flower) irises and peonies. These have all spread and grown satisfactorily into one another. The walls surrounding the garden (three brick, one stone) are almost covered with good climbing plants, including several clematis ('Gipsy Queen', 'Royal Velours' and 'Henry II') and climbing roses ('New Dawn', 'Purity' and 'Handel'). There is one very striking hydrangea, *H. sargentiana*, which has flat corymbs six to ten inches across with rose-lilac florets; also one *Magnolia × soulangeana* 'Alba Su-

perba'. Each bed is surrounded by gra walks and, in all, there are about 4 yards of grass edging to be trimmed this one garden!

Plant-association decisions are left Mr and Mrs Hornby; we agreed on th when I first came to Pusey. While consider that the garden design is im portant, I feel that too much emphasis given to the positioning of plants ar whether one plant clashes with anothe Look at the colours of the wild flowe in the countryside – Nature nev worries about the various shades leaves clashing; it is in the uncultivate country that we see true beauty.

Our greatest enemy is ground eld but we are getting the better of it ver simply. Its leaves appear and start grow before most other plants and if, soon as the leaves have uncurled, w hand-spray them with a strong mixtur of 24D weed killer and water, most of is killed.

We have lost a lot of trees – elm from elm disease and many beech after the 1976 drought – and unsight stumps were left. Mr and Mrs Hornb had the roots removed by a grinding out process, leaving a large number o wood chippings. We collected them u sprayed them with a dilute solutio of Jeyes Fluid and then stacked ther nine foot square; every six inches applied sulphate of ammonia, 4 oz pe square yard. We built the stack up to si feet high, left it for twelve months an then found that it had broken down to fine mixture, ideal for mulching som of the rose beds.

I have strong views about the lack o trace elements in soil, which leave plants more prone to disease. I try t

. Pusey House across the lake.

help, not only by feeding them with organic fertilizers such as blood, fish and bone but also by feeding them through the leaves with a leaf spray with added trace elements and, in some cases, with just trace elements. These feeds are compatible and can be mixed with most insecticides and fungicides, which means that you can mix and spray the two things at once.

All these techniques are useful in my own walled garden at Rose Cottage. It was waist high in weeds when I arrived at Pusey and underneath it all there seemed to be four sections, one piece lawn, three pieces veg. and flower garden with two long, three-foot wide cinder paths. In the first three years all I wanted to do was to get rid of the rubbish, think up a plan, re-soil, level and sow the paths with grass seed.

Along one side of the main grass path I made a larch-pole pergola trellis seven feet high and forty yards long, and then planted it with twenty-four climbing roses, some honeysuckle and clematises. I finished this twelve months ago so one can see very little progress yet. However, to cover up the poles, I have planted delphiniums the full length of the pergola, about sixty of them. I then planted sweet peas and trained them up canes; I shall not be happy, though, until I can train the roses up and along the trellis.

Hidden from the house by the pergola is the vegetable garden – this takes more time than any other aspect of gardening, mainly because of the effort to get maximum yield: from seed sowing to harvesting, every insect or sign of disease must be guarded against.

I always grow vegetables in a straight line, with a narrow path between each crop and around the outside of the garden. Plants are spaced to suit the implement I use rather than at the dis-

3.

tances recommended by the seedsman this reduces the time taken for hoeing and hand-weeding. I try to manure and dig the garden in the winter and spring at sowing time in order to get a fine tilth and, before sowing or planting, I apply an organic fertilizer such as fish, blood and bone and work it into the soil during the growing season. It is ideal to spray the plants at least twice with a liquid foliar feed as this is less wasteful than a dry feed and acts more quickly to produce better crops.

I am fortunate in that gardening is my hobby and I love every moment, as most professionals do. The old type of professional gardener, sturdily independent, is a dying breed. My old head gardener told me, long ago, about his first day in that post. The lady of the house met him in the garden and instructed him to carry out some task in the garden. He replied by removing his cap and saying, very politely, 'Begging your pardon, ma'am, but I am the head gardener and am paid to decide what to do and when to do it. All I ask of you is to walk around and enjoy the colour and tidiness we have created for you and leave us to do the work.'

4.

5.

The wonderful order of Ken Cotton's vegetable garden, screened from the house by a arch pergola, which he has recently planted with climbing roses, clematis and delphiniums.
The top end of Pusey's herbaceous border includes the red peony 'Arab Prince', while the spectacular honeysuckle *Lonicera × llmanniana* spills over the wall. 5. *Clematis* 'Perle d'Azur' covers the arch over the sundial in Lady Emily's Garden and behind the seat is *Hydrangea sargentiana*. 6. Rose Cottage, the gardener's house, overlooks Lady Emily's garden, where the double pink *Paeonia lactiflora* 'Sarah Bernhardt' glows in the evening light. 7. Behind the established floribunda rose 'Pernille Poulsen' in the border, Ken Cotton has planted the large white, sweet-scented *Nicotiana sylvestris*.

Heaselands, Haywards Heath, West Sussex

RICHARD STAPLES

Sussex is filled with good gardens and I came to this one as head gardener after many years as a landscape and garden designer. My early training had been at Logan, on the Mull of Galloway, and the Cambridge University Botanic Garden.

Firstly, I must describe my involvement with the garden at Heaselands, the thirty acres of which dominate my life. The house was built by Mr Ernest Kleinwort in 1934 and the garden has since been created progressively. He was assisted, as head gardeners, by Mr E. E. Hayes for twenty years and then by Mr T. Cowan, AHRHS, for a further twenty-one, before my arrival in 1977 shortly after Mr Kleinwort's death.

The layout of Heaselands could probably be called 'gardenesque', owing more perhaps to Repton, and possibly J. C. Loudon, than to Capability Brown. However, like most gardens, there are influences from many sources; is there such a thing as a 'pure' English garden?

Mr Kleinwort was thorough in his planning; features, planting and bord edges were marked, sometimes fo years, with his aluminium canes befo anything was constructed or plante The whole garden, which has a larg collection of hybrid rhododendrons ar azaleas, is landscaped to show off th plants to their best advantage. It is n just another collection of exotic raritie some of the plants are mundane but a so planted that their colour, texture ar shape contribute much to the beauty the whole.

In fact, plants were selected for po itions rather than the reverse. A grea deal of thought is needed before in troducing new plants into existin schemes. Mr Kleinwort's early not have plants listed under seasons (i some cases, more than one) and und colour, both foliage and flower; pr sumably his basic selections were mad from these notes.

What of my own contribution Heaselands? Much of it has involve alterations to various features an areas, often for ease of maintenanc Some cutting back, thinning or remov of plants has been necessary because plant growth; open spaces have close in and have had to be restored. Space i after all, the basic setting for plant enabling us to see them.

One of my earliest operations was redesign the herbaceous garden, twi borders 150 feet long by 10 feet wid enclosed by yew hedges. The final lay out, known as the Paved Garden, ha eight ten-foot-square beds of roses wit two thirty-foot borders, planted mainl with phlox and peonies, supplemente at present with annuals. The rest of th area is paved with York stone inset wit

1. Heaselands garden staff, left to right:
Tony Hoffman, Basil Driver, Richard Staples, Jack Tampsett, David Spink, Brian Mann and Gordon Botting.

rick panels. Seats are placed strategically, as they are throughout the garden; this, with the addition of a stone vase and a pair of figures, has created a secluded place. An arch in the yew at the west end of this enclosure leads to a circular paved area giving on to the main lawn.

Some minor alterations have been made to the Rose Garden, including the removal of standard roses (with which I am not in sympathy). Twin fastigiate yews were removed from either side of the steps so that the steps could be made fully circular. New, shallower steps have been constructed at the east end of the terrace for safety reasons and other paving areas elsewhere in the garden have been added.

A clump of *Rhododendron ponticum* by the main pond was cleared, to allow for more adventurous planting, the re-alignment of a path and the exposure of the trunks of Scots pines and a larch; tree trunks can be very attractive features.

The garden at Heaselands consists of a series of vistas which are equally attractive in either direction. This is only one of the factors that must be borne in mind when redesigning an area.

Although the colours can be bright in May and June, there is enough greenery of all shades to counteract this and to preserve the peaceful atmosphere. The garden is bisected by a valley with streamlet and ponds, man-made, and the lower part is full of bluebells. By clearing out scrub from the continuation of this valley where it is steeper-sided and more of a ghyll, it has been possible to extend the blue haze and thus enhance the springtime picture. In fact, this ghyll has great potential and perhaps, one day, it can be developed, though its naturalness is charming.

A considerable amount of new planting has been carried out in the last few years and I have tried to introduce new species, in order to extend the flowering

These steps to the terrace are among several aesthetically pleasing improvements made recently.

season of the shrubs and trees beyond May and June. In a garden, replacements are always needed and we are now having to replace flowering cherries that are beginning to die back.

This winter we have developed an area of meadow along the southern boundary, planting it initially with specimen trees which will further extend our range of plants. On the old croquet lawn we are making new azalea beds. In order to carry out these two projects we have had to give much thought to the creation of windbreaks and to integrating the new areas into the existing garden.

As to the future, I am sure we shall find room for improvements, though designing within an established garden is more difficult than starting from scratch, and one must move slowly and carefully.

Fields surround the garden of Stonepit Cottage, where we have lived since 1981, on three sides and, to the south-west, we have an oak- and pine-framed vista over the countryside to the South Downs and Chanctonbury Ring, fourteen miles away. By curving borders towards it, I have tried to accentuate this view. A seventy-foot-high fir (*Abies grandis*) on the northern side is a further focal point, beneath which are colonies of cyclamen, cowslips and bulbs; behind it I have planted azaleas.

The main borders have groups of floribunda roses, in particular 'Chanelle' and 'Rita', interplanted with shrubs and herbaceous plants; these are grouped to provide colourful displays at all times. A number of the plants are of sentimental value and have followed me from garden to garden.

On the walls of the cottage are trained *Jasminum nudiflorum*, *Pyracantha rogersiana* 'Flava', a ceanothus, rose 'New Dawn', *Berberis darwinii*, *Hydrangea petiolaris* (struggling to get going) and several clematis. In the narrow border between the path and house are *Daphne odora* 'Aureomarginata', which breaks into flower in January and is wonderfully scented,

3.

Convolvulus cneorum, Iris unguicula-ris, Lavendula spica, as well as a large-flowered hardy fuchsia, mossy saxif-rage and other herbaceous perennials. A triangular border, partially in shade, on the south side of the cottage has as its main planting my collection of ferns, in particular polystichums. I am pleased that ferns have made a comeback in recent years, as they are particularly useful for shady areas and for furnish-ing difficult spots in town gardens.

Before closing, I must pay tribute to Mrs Kleinwort's counsel, interest and constant quest for perfection, and to my staff.

Heaselands is open to the public on behalf of the National Gardens Scheme on six afternoons in May and one in July, and also to parties at other times by appointment. It is very satisfying to us that garden-lovers derive such pleasure from the result of our labours.

4.

5.

3. Richard Staples's spectacular herbaceous planting in the Paved Garden at Heaselands includes *Lavatera trimestris* 'Silver Cup' and *Nicotiana affinis.* A good-looking *Catalpa bignonioides* 'Aurea' shows above the end of the yew hedge.   4. This sympathetic flower-grouping at Stonepit Cottage is of rose 'Rita' with *Geranium psilostemon,* pinks and violas.   5. The bluebells in the valley shortly precede the flowering of *Rhododendron* 'Cynthia'.   6. Roses 'Rob Roy', 'Margaret Merrill', 'Evelyn Fison', 'Pernille Poulsen' and 'Rita' and spikes of *Eremurus bungei* in the Paved Garden; patches of thyme soften the paving.

6.

Ranger's Lodge, Hyde Park, London

ASHLEY STEPHENSON

Tourists in London come flocking to Hyde Park, particularly Speakers' Corner; the garden round Ranger's Lodge is on the north bank of the Serpentine and from the bedroom window I can watch the crowds at Speakers' Corner.

I am a professional gardener in that I am the professional head of the Royal Parks, known as the Bailiff of the Royal Parks. Ranger's Lodge is the home of the Bailiff; when retirement comes I will have to leave my home so it can be enjoyed by my successor. In consequence the garden is not exactly as I would wish to have it and changes in structure must be carefully considered as they may not fit into the character of the house or even of the park itself. Having the kind of job which often calls for a seven-day commitment I do not have as much time as I would like to do my own gardening at home.

In the course of my duties I am often called upon to meet members of my profession from all over the world, and I use my own house and garden for this rather than my office, which is in the middle of Whitehall.

Maintenance is kept to a minimum but there is no such thing as a maintenance-free garden, so there is always something to be done. When I first moved into the house there were a number of footpaths and as these did not go anywhere or do anything I removed them. This slightly increased the grass cutting but reduced greatly the edging and edge repairing, which had been a constant task. By now all signs of the paths have gone and I'm left with the circular drive, which comes in at the front of the house, and a gravel path which starts from the garage and winds its way round the bottom part of the garden. The front drive requires no maintenance as it is metalled; the gravel path gets a dose of weedkiller once a year. This was the only basic change I made; other smaller changes have been to realign rose beds and to alter slightly the shape of the borders round the garden, all in the name of making maintenance easier. Planting too has been designed so that the borders basically look after themselves, though weeding is always necessary.

The garden round Ranger's Lodge is essentially a private garden – it is not open to the public and although it can be seen from the Park it is not designed with this in mind. The difference between public park gardening and gardening round a private house is something I have to contend with every working day. In Hyde Park, close to Hyde Park Corner, is an area known as the Dell Shrubbery, with the overflow from the Serpentine – which is supplied by land drainage and by artesian wells in St James's Park – running through it. This used to be an area heavily overplanted with Victorian-type shrubs; it looked dark and uninviting, the shrubs were uninteresting and it needed a facelift. Behind the mass of evergreens the overflow from the Serpentine ran down a rocky crevasse into a narrow stream and then into a culvert down to the Thames. About ten years ago we began improving the way the water got into the stream. As the public are not admitted waterfalls had to be large enough to be viewed from the road. Work went on for years behind the screen of planting, but the structural work is now complete.

Scale is the most important difference between the two gardens; my garden, although large, is kept to personal plantings while the Dell is mass planted, as the effect has to be seen from a distance. Service paths are necessary in the Dell but they do not have to be as big as they would if the public were allowed entry. Wear is one of our big problems. Large blocks of plants are used and it is essential that these are shown to their best advantage, so the ground is tiered to lift the plantings above the surrounding clutter.

Water I consider to be a vital part of most gardens. I do however preach caution; I do not have water in my private garden as I have a granddaughter and there are many accidents in garden pools. In public areas hopefully parents are watchful and the authority has usually either protected the pool or designed it in such a way that it is not a danger. In the Dell water will give the dimension needed and it will also be possible to hear the splash of running water without there being any danger.

Because of the requirements of the job I have to spend much time at Ranger's Lodge and in consequence I enjoy my garden to the full in my spare time while being able to practise my profession during my working day.

My garden at Ranger's Lodge is, as I have already indicated, designed to be as easily managed as possible. Colour is vitally important and for this reason I have some beds where I can have seasonal bedding. The content of these beds changes from year to year, but whatever is used must last through the summer. I cannot practise change bedding, as it not only takes up a lot of time but it also means the Parks nursery, which is fully stretched, has to make special arrangements for small quantities. This year in the lawn bed I have F1 geraniums (pelargoniums), standards as well as bush varieties; the variety I have planted is 'Rose Marie', which is a lovely shade of pink. Standard fuchsias are great favourites of mine and I always allow for a number of these to be used to give height to my bedding. Geraniums and fuchsias go well together so long as you are careful about colour and form. The new forms of impatiens are, to me, some of the best of summer bedding plants; I always have a bed somewhere and this year I have used 'Grand Prix' mixed. Being able to indulge in the new varieties before they are released is one of the perks of my position; it is unwise to take anything on trust and for this reason I like to see all of the new varieties in my own garden, where I can watch their progress over the season. Many new plants do not reach the stage where they are included in the lists of plants grown for use on a wider scale. Recently 'Nell Gwyn', an Afro-French marigold, and 'Torbay Delight', an F2 geranium, have been more widely used after being tried out in my garden.

To get the best out of some garden situations it is necessary to use tubs, for often the places where plants are most needed – for clothing a wall, for example – do not have enough soil.

My first love is trees and shrubs, the plants from which one builds the character of a garden. I call it structure planting – it sets off lawns, frames the house and adds interest at all seasons.

Some of the plants in my garden are still maturing, and it is unlikely that I will still be in occupation when they are at their best. There is a magnificent weeping ash, *Fraxinus excelsior* 'Pendula', which dominates the main part of the garden; some years ago it was allowed to become overgrown, but I have cleared round it and it is assuming a good shape once again. In the same area is a sweet gum, *Liquidambar styraciflua*; this is highly regarded,

1. Ashley Stephenson relaxing on the waterfall in Regent's Park, which he began.

2.

3.

4.

5.

2. The grace-and-favour residence of Ranger's Lodge, set against a mature purple beech, is enhanced by a bed of *Pelargonium* F1 'Pink Orbit', overplanted by standards of the same variety: a border of *Cineraria maritima* 'Silver Dust' completes the bed.   3. Rose 'Doris Tysterman' providing colour as the late afternoon sun catches the leaves of a small mulberry tree.   4. Ashley Stephenson allows the western part of his garden to grow unchecked in the spring under a weeping ash: hybrid bluebells and cow parsley intermix naturally.   5. The summer planting of six tubs in front of Ranger's Lodge mainly consists of standard fuchsias underplanted with pelargoniums and the silver foliage of *Helichrysum petiolatum*.

ainly because of its autumn colour-
ag. The English cherry, *Prunus avium*,
aust be fifty feet tall; unfortunately,
ecause of crowding round the base, it
ost all its lower branches. The birds
njoy the fruits each year. My favourite
ree in the garden is *Acer japonicum*
'Aconitifolium' – its leaves are a great
oy. It too had been overcrowded, and
although I have cleared round it it is still
 one-sided tree, but it should improve
vith time. A copper beech tree to the
orth of the house has been falling
own during the thirty years I have
nown it. On at least three occasions it
as been propped up and on each occa-
ion the props began to bend. Last year I
ad the tree lightened, which should
nsure that it lasts me out; its colouring
s a source of much pleasure.

Smaller trees include *Prunus* 'Kur-
ar', *P. subhirtella* 'Autumnalis' and a
nake bark maple, *Acer hersii*. In the
nain lawn is a mulberry which is well
over thirty years old but still shows no
ign of flowering or fruiting.

Some of the better shrubs in the
garden are *Photinia* 'Red Robin', *Cotinus coggygria*, better known as the
smoke bush, *Garrya elliptica*, which is
one of the nicest of all winter-interest
shrubs, and *Mahonia bealei*, with its
yellow, sweetly scented flowers in
January. The witch hazel, *Hamamelis
mollis*, also flowers in January and the
choisya displays its white blossoms in
the early summer. Diervilla, weigela,
philadelphus, cotoneaster, viburnum,
senecio and berberis give variation in
leaf form and colour over the year.
Especially nice are *Magnolia liliflora*
'Nigra' and the beauty bush, *Kolkwitzia
amabilis*; they are completely different
but are both ideal garden plants.

Camellias do extremely well – fifteen-
foot bushes flower profusely each spring.
I also have a few rhododendrons despite the fact that the pH of the soil is
close to 7; *Rhododendron* 'Polar Bear' is
one, and dwarf forms include 'Carlew',
'Bow Bells' and 'Elizabeth'.

My garden is not a showpiece; it is
the place where I relax away from the
pressures of work.

6. Early autumn under the chestnuts, looking towards the mature sycamore, *Acer pseudoplatanus*.

137

Anglesey Abbey, Lode, Cambridgeshire

RICHARD AYRES

East Anglian meadow and farmland surround the twelfth-century Anglesey Abbey, flat fields reaching as far as the eye can see. From such country, a twentieth-century garden has been created – a hundred acres of avenues, sweeping lawns and parkland, with smaller areas like a rose garden, a formal hyacinth garden and a pinetum.

The first Lord Fairhaven, who began this project in 1930, was not primarily a plantsman; his real interest was in producing an effect, which he would often heighten by the careful placing of a piece of classical sculpture or a garden ornament, of which he amassed a large collection.

My father was head gardener at Anglesey and on Lord Fairhaven's instructions he set about digging out the causeway around Quarry Pool; this was quite an achievement before the days of JCBs and one of which he was justly proud. Now it is possible to stand back by the second-century Roman altar under the limes on one side of the pool and look across through a space in the

1. Richard Ayres and the south front of Anglesey Abbey.

willow trees to a vista with, as its focal point, a herm of Pan behind a seat on the other side. From another point, the pool, deliberately kept clear of water lilies, reflects the Roman altar among the willows.

Nobody visiting Anglesey can fail to be impressed by the many avenues of trees, another of Lord Fairhaven's passions. I remember as a boy thinking that the trees of the Lime Avenue should have been planted closer together; now, forty years on, we must decide whether to let them grow together or to take every other one out. As it is, we have already drastically thinned the half mile of chestnut trees which my father planted in 1937 and which became Coronation Avenue.

Soon after I took over from my father, Dutch elm disease started to take its toll in the garden; it was heartbreaking. Some of the 4,500 elms must have been over three hundred years old and, with rookeries high in their branches, were looked on by my father as old friends. It was very hard for me to instigate the felling of these giants but the work was accomplished as speedily as possible through the skilled and devoted work of the five gardeners and with the generous financial support of the National Trust, who now own the estate.

A massive replanting programme was undertaken. We now have limes (*Tilia cordata* and *T. platyphyllos* 'Rubra', the red-twigged lime), beeches (*Fagus sylvatica*), oaks (*Quercus cerris*, the Turkey oak, *Q. ilex*, the holm or evergreen oak, and *Q. robur*, the common oak), alders (*Alnus cordata*), and willows (*Salix alba*) together with un-

usual trees and shrubs along the fringe of the shelter belts to add variety and colour.

The most recent avenue to be planted runs parallel to the back drive; formerly Daffodil Walk, its elms used to be a magnificent sight, especially at daffodil time and again in May, when a sea of cow parsley flowered on either side. The elm disease and eelworm in the daffodils defeated our attempts to restock it, however, so we cleared the whole lot and planted a hornbeam avenue (*Carpinus betulus*) there in 1977. To commemorate Her Majesty the Queen's Silver Jubilee it was renamed Jubilee Avenue.

The arboretum contains many trees of merit. The Hungarian oak, *Quercus frainetto*, will probably be one of our most notable trees in years to come; looking at its height and spread now it is difficult to realize that it is still less than sixty years old. Another lime, *Tilia oliverii*, is a firm favourite of mine; medium sized, with light green leaves whose undersides are almost grey in spring, it is a fine picture in the breeze.

The mature tulip tree (*Liriodendron tulipifera*), which bears tulip-like flowers in July, has never really appealed to me. I much prefer the delicate, very small red-stamened flowers of the *Parrotia persica* in early spring or the Judas tree (*Cercis siliquastrum*), covered in deep pink blossom in June – that's a tree we could do with more of at Anglesey.

Many of my favourite trees are much older, having been planted by the owner of around 1860, the Reverend John Hailstone: *Sequoiadendron giganteum* (how visitors like to bash the rubbery bark!), two majestic cedars (*Cedrus*

Irish ivy (*Hedera hibernica*) forms a path under mature Atlas cedars (*Cedrus atlantica* 'Glauca').

tlantica) and a very good specimen of the weeping silver lime (*Tilia petiolaris*), the scent from which is magnificent in early summer.

Nearer the house, I get much satisfaction from working on the herbaceous border, which was originally designed by Major Daniell, a friend of Lord Fairhaven. The border comes into its own in July with a beauty which never fails to overawe me. Some of our delphiniums (the best is 'Sonata'), with stems individually staked and tied at least three times, grow to over ten feet. During growth, as soon as they are big enough, the shoots are 'plucked', to leave no more than five strong shoots per plant; lined out in a nursery bed, the discarded shoots will make new plants in twelve months.

With the delphiniums we have *Thalictrum glaucum, Campanula lactiflora, Achillea filipendulina* 'Gold Plate', *Galega officinalis* 'Alba' and 'Lady Wilson', and a seedling verbascum introduced by Major Daniell. *Dictamnus fraxinella*, the burning bush, grows well, both the pink and white-flowering cultivars, and the

lemon scent is superb, especially after rain.

Rabbits are the scourge of my life. They devour large chunks of heliopsis and erigerons, and some years they sit and eat every flower bud of the pyrethrums. A built-in clock must tell them when it is five o'clock and time for the gardeners to go. Because of the rabbits we have to place wire-netting along the dahlia beds during the growing season. The Dahlia Garden adjoins the Herbaceous Garden and takes the form of a long, curving, beech-bordered grass corridor, with a marble statue of Apollo recessed in the hedge. All along the outside of the curve, whose full extent is never seen, is set a wide bed which, in spring, doubles as the forget-me-not garden. Thirty cultivars of tall dahlias (poms, cactus and decoratives) make a splendid show in August and September.

Storing the tubers through the winter is a problem and our best results come from storing them in clamps. Each clamp begins with a good coat of dry straw on the ground, then the dahlia tubers placed round a wire funnel

and then another good coat of straw round the sides and over the top, leaving the funnel open. We then finish with a good six inches of soil all round and a prayer to the Almighty that all will be well in the spring.

One of our crowning achievements each year must be the formal Hyacinth Garden, made just before the war; imagine the scent from four and a half thousand blue and white hyacinths ('Ostara' and 'L'Innocence') in this geometrical garden. The bulbs are planted in October (after lifting masses of red and yellow bedding dahlias) and, depending on the winter, they flower about mid-April. When the flowers begin to fade, we pluck the florets by drawing the hand up the stem to stop them seeding. The bulbs are left in the beds until the first week in June when they are lifted and cleaned, the tops removed and the bulbs stored on racks until the autumn.

The present Lord Fairhaven, who lives at Anglesey with his family, is rightly very eager to maintain the high standards set by his uncle; the Rose Garden is part of his private garden and

contains some thousand roses arrange
formally in beds. We are continuall
improving the varieties while main
taining the most interesting of the old
the pale yellow 'Sir Henry Segrave', th
deep salmon 'Angels Mateu', the ver
pale pink 'Caroline Testout' and th
white 'Frau Karl Druschki'. This la
has all its last year's shoots pegge
down to a frame a foot above the be
which encourages it to flower freel
from the leaf axils. Some of our mor
recent introductions have been 'Ernes
H. Morse' (red), 'Basildon Bond' (apr
cot) and 'Silver Jubilee' (salmon pink).

My own one third of an acre garden i
mostly lawn around some good-qualit
fruit trees; I also thoroughly enjo
growing vegetables. The shaped bed
around the lawn contain mainly shrub
and conifers with a sprinkling of choic
herbaceous plants.

Whether at the Abbey or in my ow
garden, one of the great joys of being
gardener is in the sense of looking for
ward. Every month, even in winter
there are plants and trees at their best
but perhaps our greatest contribution
here has been the planting of the trees
these will enrich our gardens for year
to come.

3.

4.

3. Mixed daffodils in the Monks' Garden.
4. In this small part of the vast, semicircular
herbaceous border, backlit by the evening sun,
acanthus buds, centranthus, rudbeckia, achillea,
lychnis and thalictrum mass together with, in
the centre, *Salvia sclarea turkestanica*, one of
Richard Ayres's favourite plants.   5. Richard
Ayres's father planted Coronation Avenue, a
half mile of chestnut trees, in 1937, which Lord
Fairhaven commemorated with this ten-foot urn
set in a circle of silver birches.   6. The marble
statue of Apollo, recessed into the beech hedge o
the Dahlia Garden, looks out on to thirty
different cultivars of fully grown dahlias.
7. Four and a half thousand blue and white
hyacinths make up the Hyacinth Garden, and are
later replaced by bedding dahlias.
8. *Carpenteria californica* in full flower on the
Abbey's south front.

5.

6.

7.

8.

University Botanic Gardens, St Andrews, Fife

ROBERT J. MITCHELL

Visitors to gardens invariably find plenty of interest – new ideas, new plants, new concepts. The climate and location play a major role in the determination of what *can* be grown, and the teaching and research requirements of any botanic garden largely determine what *should* be grown.

In St Andrews the teaching covers a wide spectrum of subjects from taxonomy and ecology, through genetics, physiology and biochemistry, to plant pathology and mycology. Thus a huge range of the plant kingdom is required and there are currently about six or seven thousand taxa in the garden and glasshouses.

St Andrews cannot boast an ancient Botanic Garden, but it is justly proud of being the first Scottish University, founded in 1411. The Botanic Garden dates from 1889 when Dr John Wilson laid out order beds according to the Bentham and Hooker classification. A year later the Department of Botany was founded as a separate department. Development in the original garden continued till 1960 when a new site of 18.5 acres was taken back from a tenant farmer and market gardener.

The site, which slopes to the north, has major contours, a beautiful backdrop of mature trees and a stream on the northern boundary which is shared with the District Council. The soil is a rich medium loam with a heavy clay subsoil on the upper part of the site and a sandy gravel subsoil on the lower northern part adjacent to the stream. With a pH of 7.14 derived from the local magnesium limestone, the soil can be adapted to suit a wide range of plants.

The early plans of the garden were centred on producing the correct habitats for the large collection built up during the previous seventy years, so peat, rock and water gardens were constructed; tree and shrub borders were planted on the periphery of the garden to provide shelter and screening; herbaceous borders were planted in the semi-formal areas and island beds in more informal settings; bulb borders, which also include tender shrubs, were positioned around the glasshouse range where they could be easily maintained and coddled; and an order bed system was designed and laid out in the Cronquist/Takhtajan classification, which is based on evolutionary trends in the plant kingdom.

The underlying pattern is to grow plants where they will grow best. Ecological collections of Scottish native plants are being gathered together in a series of groupings from serpentine fellfield, limestone pavement and high mountain plants to lowland fen and meadow plants, giving the student and visitor recognizable plant associations. For this, soil pH and structure have been altered to provide these special growing conditions – in some cases with soil and rock brought from serpentine and limestone areas. The pH is altered to suit plants which require acid soil by using peat and annual dressings of flowers of sulphur.

In the cold east coast of Scotland, shelter is the main consideration when planning a garden, and at the first opportunity in 1962 a mixed conifer plantation was planted on the western boundary. Hedging was placed to separate the public garden from the research

1. Robert Mitchell.

rea and these hedges of Leyland cypress, beech and myrobalan plum now give good shelter from the east. With the demise of the coastal railway line, further trees have been planted on the eastern boundary to give shelter from the salt-laden winds of winter. Tree and shrub borders were planned to run across the direction of the prevailing winds, thus giving further shelter and providing microclimates throughout the garden.

The central area extending to the northern boundary is occupied by the rock garden and ponds and, to the east of this and set into a bank, nestling beside a pine copse, is the peat garden, with its borders and peat walls.

My interest in plants, encouraged by my grandfather – an amateur grower of some repute – stems from the age of two or thereabouts. This developed into a love of hill-walking among the Border hills. It is impossible to walk among the cliffs and screes and not to notice the structure of the rock and the plants, which change with soil type and altitude. This interest has been a considerable joy, as it is to all gardeners, when visiting other countries. For me, exploring the mountain ranges of British Columbia and Oregon and leading a team of botanists and horticulturists in Western Yunnan in 1981 in a joint botanical expedition with Chinese botanists are particularly memorable.

Gardeners attempt to emulate in gardens the growing conditions they have seen in the wild. To make a garden which looks natural and aesthetically pleasing yet still provides the correct conditions for plants has been our challenge and our delight. The way cliffs erode, producing scree which then modifies to moorland, or meadow to bog and water is not easy to imitate in a garden. Neither is it an easy task to blend an alkaline rock feature with acid peat wall areas in the space of a few yards. We have used the heath and heather garden with its outcrops of rock and mini peat walls to act as the pivotal feature to achieve this, with *Juniperus communis* 'Hibernica' and *Pinus mugo* to give a

partial screen and shelter for the more vulnerable and wind-tender plants.

The rock garden contains plants from the high mountain ranges of the world from the Arctic to the Andes, from Bhutan to Basutoland, from New Zealand to Newfoundland, not forgetting our own natives such as *Silene acaulis, Dryas octopetala, Juniperus communis nana, Lychnis alpina*, and so on.

When planning the garden, ever mindful that the teaching terms are during the least floriferous time of year, we have tried to find and grow plants with a long flowering season or, in particular, winter- and spring-flowering species. It is possible to have flowers all the year round in the garden. One of the most floriferous rock garden plants is *Viola correvoniana* – a plant selected at Correvon's nursery in Switzerland – which flowers for ten months of the year. Its large, pale blue flowers are always a joy to see. There are crevice plants – ramondas, haberleas, lewisias and so on, growing beside campanulas, hebes, daphnes, saxifrages and erinus; dwarf and slow-growing conifers, which carpet the ground or act as a foil, provide shelter and scale to the layout. European primulas and androsaces grow well in the well-drained situations, and dwarf *Geranium* and *Erodium* species enjoy the sunny, exposed places.

Bulbs, pulsatillas and saxifrages provide the early flourish in the spring, while *Cyclamen hederifolium* and *Kniphofia galpinii* flower in the autumn.

There are no real specialities in the range of plants. It is simply a collection of as wide a spectrum of plant families as is possible, to flower and be available for the teaching purpose of the garden.

There are three different aspects of landscaping used in the garden. Overall, it was planned to look aesthetically exciting with rounded borders containing plants with similar cultural requirements grouped together and, in the tree and shrub borders, three or four tiers of plants from tall trees to ground cover utilizing the space to maximum effect.

In other areas, especially those concerned with the Scottish native plants, a series of ecological plantings have been developed, using wild source material. Lastly, the teaching value of order beds has been maintained and developed in the new classification and although most of the plants flourish during the summer months, there is enough in flower during term times to enable students to study the classification of plants. In addition, flowers are collected during the growing season and put into deep freeze till teaching starts again.

The development of the new Botanic Garden has taken sixteen years to complete – but no garden is ever complete and already alterations are under way. It is thus a never-ending joy in creativity, more often than not to the detriment of other activities.

My own garden has in the past been a source of amusement to my friends, for there seemed a great lack of effort in its upkeep due to lack of time. It is, however, maturing now and is virtually self-maintaining, apart from the occasional tidy-up and replanting. It has been designed to look well at all seasons, with an abundance of evergreen shrubs and with plants in flower most of the year.

It is a relaxation to work in my own garden, simply to potter about with no deadlines to keep; one aim is to provide an interesting range of plants which can be viewed from the roadside. I abhor hedges but I need privacy, so shrubs have been planted to provide that screen and also give interest to the passer-by. Plants range from the wind-hardy *Olearia haastii* and *Viburnum tinus* to *Salix melanostachys* with its unusual black catkins and the butterfly-attracting *Buddleia* 'Lochinch'. Behind this screen alpines predominate, set against a background of senecio, *Santolina chamaecyparissus*, hebe and *Genista hispanica*. Taller plants lift the height – these include *Rosa omiensis pteracantha*, pruned hard each year to produce those marvellous spines, and *Parrotia persica* and *Euonymus elatus*, two of the best autumn-colouring plants in this area.

2.

Treasures include a collection of rhododendrons (which have to be coddled in the dry east coast but they do well with added irrigation) and plants introduced from China by our expedition in 1981. Those include *Incarvillea mairei*, *Gentiana ternifolia* and a host of *Philadelphus*, *Deutzia*, *Berberis* and *Hypericum* species. Wherever I look, whether it is from the seat at the window or pottering in the garden, all the plants bring back memories. That is what gardening is all about though, is it not?

2. Looking towards the rock garden from the largest pond with *Hosta sieboldii* in the foreground and *Carex pendula* and *scirpus* (rushes) beyond.   3. The Botanic Garden's island beds include beautiful grasses, in particular the purple plumes of *Calamagrostis curtonus paniculata* and the golden *Stipa gigantea*.   4. *Aethionema arabicum*, *Chamaecyparis pisifera* 'Filifera Aurea', *Iris japonica*, *Daphne cneorum* 'Eximia' and *Alyssum montanum* form the foreground to this view through the rock garden. Conifers in the middle distance include *Chamaecyparis lawsoniana* 'Minima Glauca', *Juniperus communis* 'Cracow', *Juniperus recurva coxii* and *Abies koreana*.   5. Part of the scree and rock garden in spring: in the foreground, the grey foliage of *Andryala aghardii* and the yellow flowers of *Saxifraga conifera* contrast with the weathering whinstones set into the scree.   6. A fine patch of *Primula vialii* in the peat garden.

3

4.

5.

6.

Harewood House, Leeds, Yorkshire

ALAN MASON

It's one thing to be a professional gardener and advise other people on what they should and should not do in their gardens. It's quite another thing deciding what should be done in your own garden.

Patsy, my wife, and I and our two small children live in a large detached house on the Harewood Estate, with a garden on a north-facing slope.

When we first moved in my intention was that the house should be surrounded by an old English cottage garden but, apart from imagining hollyhocks around the windows, I always seemed to be unable to form a complete picture of it in my mind. After a period of several months of inactivity I realized I had failed to sort out the cottage garden that I had initially felt to be so right, and that a different line of thinking was therefore required.

1. Alan Mason.

The garden originally had a sloping lawn with a rose border at the bottom, which had been levelled out, near the house. In the lawn was a cherry (never my favourite tree) and a lilac.

I decided to remove both the trees, and as the roses were old they could come out at the same time.

From the house it was possible to see everything which had been growing on this slope at one viewing. I decided that this would have to change – half the fun of a garden is discovering what's around the corner, out of sight.

When I had ploughed up the old grass and tired rose bed, the top of the slope was levelled out; this was to be a lawn – too high up to be seen from the house. In an effort to create an air of mystery a 'statue' (part of a monument previously dismantled on the estate) was positioned at one end of the lawn-to-be.

Being a gardener does seem to mean that I spend a lot of time everywhere except my own garden. I must admit, however, to having a pride in my 'top lawn'; I always try to find ten minutes two or three times a week to mow the lawn and edge it and I maintain that this is the best bit of lawn on the whole estate. I have always had a keen interest in lawns, and this tiny stretch just allows me to keep my hand in. This lawn is at the top of the slope furthest away from the house and the main part of the garden slopes down from the lawn towards the house; this needed to be broken up to create some interest, as well as access.

This was achieved by making a couple of meandering paths, one in gravel across the largest bed and another in thyme from the top lawn to the house.

The idea here was that the path, planted with variegated *Thymus* 'Doone Valley', would be interesting to look at and scented when walked on. That was the theory – in practice the daisies grew quicker than the thyme and I didn't get enough time to weed it properly.

The planting of the garden, apart from the basic skeleton of conifers and rhododendrons, has been a try-it-and-see affair. Generally I built up groups of plants, rather than plant things as single specimens; I tried to get each plant to look well next to its neighbours, using contrast of colour and form of foliage as one of the most important requisites – very often the flowers were a secondary consideration. I like to extend the season and interest of plants and to grow something like a honeysuckle through a shrub such as *Physocarpus opulifolius* 'Luteus' to show off the flowers of the honeysuckle against the yellow foliage of the physocarpus.

This is still a very young garden and I frequently look at a patch of the garden and think 'That will have to go next year' or 'I ought to alter that just a little.' This to me is one of the important things about gardening; it's not simply a case of drawing up a plan and design and thereafter sticking rigidly to the original idea. Gardens develop and evolve over a period – new ideas emerge and need to be brought into the existing pattern of planting so that the need combines happily with what is already established.

That is also the case when developing areas of the Harewood House grounds. It would be disastrous when opening up and developing new areas if no consideration were given to the already nature and historically important gardens. Lady Harewood is particularly interested in the gardens and likes to discuss the future of various areas. She was most concerned, when the idea was first aired of a woodland garden as an entrance to the lakeside walks, that this should be in keeping with the surrounding area. After fairly lengthy discussion and interchange of ideas this garden was started and now splendidly complements the rest of the grounds.

The involvement of Lord and Lady Harewood was again particularly important when it was decided to reinstate on the terrace a section of the Italian-style parterre, to the original design by Nesfield. This job proved to be great fun, looking at old photographs and plans to ensure that, as far as possible, the design was successfully re-created. The terrace itself has been used to good effect by utilizing its south-facing wall as a backing for a recently planted mixed herbaceous border. Up until then only a few shrubs grew in the grass here on the archery lawn by the wall. The Archery Border was created and the shrubs now seem much more at home, complemented by the more colourful plantings which now surround them.

Another area to be given a facelift was the dell or rock garden. This area had been planted out previously but had become overgrown and was closed to the public. This always seemed a great pity, because it is only from inside this sunken garden that the waterfall (over-spill from the Capability Brown lake) can be seen. We spent most of one winter chopping down and removing brambles, nettles and other choice exotic weeds; the following summer we battled hard to try and hold the weeds back. After this initial period of confrontation a tremendous amount of new planting has taken place – especially of rhododendrons, primulas, hostas and astilbes. We house the National Collection of both Hostas and Astilbes. Our collection of hostas is complementary to that of Wisley.

Much easier to develop was the garden of old-fashioned roses in front of the bothy, which has done remarkably well in only three years. Tremendous growth has taken place – some of the roses have made sizeable shrubs and the climbing form of the rose 'Constance Spry' is doing a splendid job in covering eight-foot tall frames and adding height to the garden. Although the garden backs on to a wall and has a southern aspect, I think one of the major reasons for its success has been the mulching with spent hops from a local brewery. This has kept the moisture in the soil during dry spells and has done a first-rate job of keeping out annual weeds.

In stark contrast to anything else in the grounds, the most recently developed area is the Yorkshire Television

. A section of the long herbaceous border in front of Harewood House.

Garden, a rectangular plot of 30 × 6
feet with its own small greenhouse an
potting-shed. It is used for programme
presented by Marylyn Webb, of 'YT
Calendar', and myself, showing ho
the knowledge gained from a larg
stately home garden can be put to goo
use in the average-size garden. This i
tremendously popular with the visitin
public, as it is something that they ca
relate to their own home gardens.

3. The original Nesfield parterre on the terrace
of Harewood House was recreated in 1982 and is
here bedded out with begonias.   4. The rock
garden, or Dell, full of established rhododendror
was cleared and opened again in 1981. In the fore
ground are *Primula pulverulenta* and
Gunnera manicata.   5. The Archery Border
(so called because the long lawn was
once used for archery) was created in 1981
as a mixed border for roses, perennials and
annuals.   6. The Bothy Rose Garden was
created in 1982; the rose 'Constance Spry'
climbs on pyramids of trellis which were
specially built for it.   7. In Alan Mason's
garden the statue has *Hedera* 'Cloth of Gold'
around it and *Dianthus* 'Mrs Sinkins' flowers in
the bed beyond.   8. Alan Mason's lawn in his
own garden winds around the mixed plantings
he enjoys.

3.

4.

5

7.

8.

Acknowledgements

Jerry Harpur thanks all the contributors for their immense help in the preparation of *The Gardener's Garden*, and in particular the Professional Gardeners' Guild, the work of fourteen of whose members is included: Messrs Akers, Anderton, Barnes, Beagley, Beasley, Borlase, Eason, Hall, Hutchinson, Lovatt, Macfadyen, Mason, Pearson and Staples.

Others who gave invaluable advice include John Sales (National Trust), Eric Robson (National Trust for Scotland), Dick Shaw (Royal Botanic Garden, Edinburgh), Jane Brown, Beth Chatto, Mervyn Feesey, Elspeth Napier, David Papworth and Rosemary Verey.

Doreen Dawson (who also made the index), Terry Illsley, Jim Marshall (National Trust), John Nicholls, Tim Rees and Anne Stevens provided editorial assistance. Downtown Darkroom made the black and white prints.

Jerry Harpur also wishes to thank Michael Dover, who originally took up the idea of *The Gardener's Garden*, Eleo Gordon, who guided the book through all its stages, and Bet Ayer, who has designed it so beautifully.

Index

Page numbers in **bold** refer to illustrations